The Kennet & Avon Canal

A User's Guide to the Waterways
between Reading and Bristol

Niall Allsop

Millstream Books

To the memory of
MARTIN and JOHN KNILL
a singular couple
whose humanity and humour
will ever touch those who knew them

Cover illustrations:
The wooded splendour of the Limpley Stoke valley
contrasting with the magic of Bath's Sydney Gardens

First published 1987; second edition 1989; third edition 1992; fourth edition 1999

Millstream Books
18 The Tyning
Bath BA2 6AL

This book is set in Helvetica Neue and Sabon

Printed in Great Britain by The Matthews Wright Press, Chard

© Niall Allsop 1987, 1989, 1992, 1999

ISBN 0 948975 28 8

Introduction

On a sharp Good Friday morning in 1982 Kay Bowen and I slowly coaxed our narrowboat home, *Dolly*, into the bottom lock of Bath's Widcombe flight. We had wintered both in the controlled waters of Bristol's Floating Harbour and on the unpredictable Avon at Bath and, with the dramas of recent flooding on the latter fresh in our minds, were grateful for having stumbled upon the re-opening of the Kennet & Avon between Bath and Dundas.

The mood was festive. Cameras clicked; eyes, strained and straining, peered over the edge of each lock chamber at boats flaunting their brass and bunting. A day to be remembered. But it was, above all else, a day memorable in the lasting friendships it spawned – with Tony Jackson who later bought *Dolly*, with Tim and Wendy Wheeldon who were to re-open part of the Somersetshire Coal Canal and with erstwhile canal carriers, John and Martin Knill – and one, almost obsessional relationship … with the Kennet & Avon.

I should, I suppose, have seen it coming. During the previous 15 years I had, after all, lived in Reading, Bradford-on-Avon, Bath and Bristol and within a few miles of Hungerford, Pewsey, Devizes and Semington. For years the Kennet & Avon and its bridges had been an incessant, sinuous and largely derelict factor in my day-to-day routines.

My journey through these pages has all but exorcised my obsession; by tramping over old ground and re-discovering past haunts I have put the Kennet & Avon in perspective; form and force have become reconciled. That is not to say that I won't continue to extol its beauty, wonder at its boldness, revel in its restoration … and be moved by one short but very special length.

My hope is that the reader – boater, walker or armchair enthusiast – will likewise be moved to venture onto the water or towpath, to be guided through the delights of the Kennet & Avon Canal between Reading and Bristol … and in so doing perhaps understand why I have resisted the fashionable temptation to rename it, in the interests of strictest accuracy, the Kennet & Avon Navigation, Kennet & Avon Waters or the Kennet & Avon Waterway.

Acknowledgements

I should especially like to thank Kay Bowen for her support, patience, advice and, with this fourth edition, typing; Tony Jackson for wheels, wisdom and *Dolly*; Tim Wheeldon for his accumulated knowledge and his willingness to share it.

Thanks also to Harry Bell, Jenny and Bob Butler, Bob Evans, Bill Fisher, Wendy Furey, Tim Graham, Will Jackson, Terry Kemp, the late Sir John Knill, Ian Mackintosh, Ken Taylor and Nick Wright for their combined wisdom, Steve Chandler for his black & white processing, and Alan Summers for his line drawings.

Grateful thanks to Imray, Laurie, Norie and Wilson for permission to quote extracts from Montague and Ann Lloyd's *Through England's Waterways*.

Past into Present

Rivers are a part of the natural order of things and as such have been increasingly subject to man's controlling instincts – either as a source of food or power or as a means of transport. During and from the Middle Ages attempts to make rivers navigable tended to conflict with the long-held 'rights' of mill-owners to dam and otherwise manipulate the flow to power their mills and even to farm fish. Recent research has suggested that such dams and by-pass leats could have their origins in earlier Roman navigations which, it is argued, were not an uncommon feature of Britain's 3rd-century landscape. Such chicken-and-egg arguments, however, would scarcely have appeased the 18th-century mill-owners who were faced with proposals to make navigable the rivers Kennet and Avon.

The idea of an east-west waterways link was first mooted in Elizabethan times, but despite the inherent 'logic' in a subsequent scheme of the 1660s which made much of the fact that, at one point, the Avon and the Thames were a mere three miles apart, nothing happened until the early 18th century. The two schemes that did bear fruit – to make the rivers Kennet and Avon navigable – did so to meet local needs and, therefore, independently of each other.

Though there had been more frequent rumblings about making the Avon navigable from Hanham Mills to Bath, it was proposals for the Kennet Navigation that were the first to be completed. The Bill introduced into Parliament in 1708 had the support of towns such as Hungerford, Trowbridge and Bradford-on-Avon while Reading was less enthusiastic, fearing the loss of status and trade. Nor were mill-owners between Reading and Newbury enamoured with the project which eventually received the Royal Assent in 1715. The $18^1/_2$-mile navigation – $11^1/_2$ miles of new cut and 7 miles of river with a rise/fall of 134ft through 20 turf-sided locks – took nine years to complete under the supervision of its surveyor-engineer, John Hore.

In no way did the completion of works in 1724 lessen the arguments or the distrust, particularly among Reading's bargemen and the Kennet's mill-owners. Sabotage and threatening letters resulted in recriminations and financial insecurity for some 40 years until, under the influence of one Francis Page, improvements to the navigation brought in their wake a semblance of stability and profitability.

Meanwhile, under pressure from many local businessmen, the Avon was made navigable from Hanham Mills to Bath – $11^1/_2$ miles through six locks. The first cargo of "Deal boards, Pig-Lead and Meal" arrived in Bath in December 1727, three-and-a-half years after the inauguration of works under the direction of John Hore. Hore's connection with both river navigations was coincidental – other than in his reputation as an able engineer; indeed, at the time he was working on the Avon he was in dispute with his erstwhile employers on the Kennet.

Blake's Lock at Reading, clearly at one with its attendant hostelry and housing while the individuality of the navigation's sole surviving turf-sided lock, Garston, is strongly protected by a war-time pillbox.

From the start, the Avon Navigation fared better than the Kennet and soon barge-loads of Shropshire coal upstream, and Bath stone downstream (hauled, incidentally, by men, not horses), were commonplace; the former displeased the Somerset colliers who, it is widely believed, were the 'Persons unknown' who destroyed Saltford Lock in 1738, while the latter furthered the business activities of one of the Navigation's shareholders, Ralph Allen.

Although ideas of eastward extension to gain access to the upper Avon's cloth-making towns such as Bradford-on-Avon and Chippenham were mooted, not even the towns involved seemed especially interested – besides which such works were seen purely in terms of extending navigation along the river. All that changed in 1788 when westward extension of the Kennet Navigation was discussed by interested parties who, at their second meeting, realised that any such scheme would gain more support if it were to unite the two extant Navigations. The so-called Western Canal project was born.

A triumvirate of surveyors favoured a Newbury-Bath link via Hungerford, Ramsbury, Marlborough, Calne, Chippenham, Lacock, Melksham and Bradford-on-Avon while a fourth, Robert Whitworth, suspected the adequacy of such a route's water supply. Through his connections with the Earl of Ailesbury, John Rennie was called in and it was his 1790 assessment – that there was an adequate water supply – that consolidated the Committee's resolve.

But the time was not right. The mania that had swept the north took time to work its way south and when it did the Western Canal Committee was ready. In 1793 they commissioned a further survey from Rennie and it was his change of mind – that the proposed canal should follow a more southerly route through Great Bedwyn, Devizes and Trowbridge – that begat the new name, the Kennet & Avon Canal. Thus, on 17th April 1794, 'An Act for making a Navigable Canal from the River Kennet, at or near the Town of Newbury, in the County of Berks, to the River Avon, at or near the City of Bath; and also certain Navigable Cuts therein described …' received the Royal Assent as the Kennet & Avon Canal Act.

It was over 16 years later, with completion of the Caen Hill locks at Devizes, that the final link in the Bath-Newbury chain was forged. Financial and construction difficulties caused delays and setbacks; Rennie's route was found wanting (hence the tendency today to sing his praises as a canal architect rather than as a surveyor) and the monies saved by opting for a shorter summit level resulted in continual – and continuing – water supply problems.

From 1796 the Kennet & Avon Canal Company had a majority shareholding in the Avon Navigation and though it never gained outright control it did initiate the long-overdue horse towing-path by 1812. Its acquisition in the same year of the Kennet Navigation, gave it, to all intents and purposes, control of all navigation between Hanham Mills and Reading. Coincidentally in 1803 'An Act for Improving and rendering

While Padworth Lock exchanges the indignity of dereliction for a concrete overcoat, Monkey Marsh exudes a kind of beauty from the depths of decay.

more Commodious the Port and Harbour of Bristol' became law; work began the following year and what became known as the Floating Harbour was completed in 1809.

Thus, by the end of the first decade of the 19th century, the stage was set for the fullest exploitation of cheaper and regular 'imports' of raw material and fuel and the 'export' of local produce, including a direct link to and from the ports of London and Bristol.

But neither time nor technology stands still and that same inquisitiveness and inventiveness that fired the early canal engineers was relentless in its pursuit of further refinements. The Railway Age thus followed close on the heels of the Canal Age and by 1841 the Great Western Railway had provided their own alternative London-Bristol link, the beginning of the end of the Kennet & Avon as a major east-west commercial artery. In 1852 the K&ACC sold the canal, the Kennet Navigation and their interests in the Avon Navigation to the GWR (who later gained outright control of the Avon) with the proviso that the navigation be maintained as such.

To leap forward a century is to stumble upon a canal coming to terms with its death throes with resourceful and persistent carriers such as John Knill of Braunston and John Gould of Newbury facing up to the inevitable. Curiously, GWR ownership seems to have prolonged the canal's active life; the K&A's two connecting waterways, the narrow Somersetshire Coal and Wilts & Berks Canals, found their trade drastically curtailed by railway competition and closed in 1904 and 1906 respectively. The closures naturally had repercussions for the K&A and trade in 1906 was described thus: "speaking generally, the actual traffic on the Kennet & Avon at the western end would not exceed more than about three or four boats a day, and on the higher levels at the eastern end it would not average one a day". And yet the canal did survive and, before decay and dereliction finally set in, almost made that psychological leap from carrying goods to carrying people which proved to be the only way forward for the vast majority of Britain's remaining waterways.

That is not to say that the canal had never embraced the concept of boating for pleasure and/or passenger-carrying; on the contrary, despite its goods-carrying origins, the K&A's man-made and natural assets had always attracted the carrying of a human cargo. Even before the Avon Navigation was fully open a passenger service was inaugurated between Bristol and Twerton. By 1730 there was a daily wherry service between Bath and Bristol; ten years on, there were two boats making the 4-hour trip daily at a fare of one shilling. Similarly, when the Bath to Bradford-on-Avon section was first opened a passenger service was quickly established. Run by John Andreas, it was used by the K&ACC for its 1808 tour of inspection and subsequently described in the *Bath Chronicle* as an "elegant packet boat".

In 1833 the spectre of railway competition prompted the K&ACC and others to investigate the claims attributed to a new breed of boat from Scotland:

A family outing at Newbury Lock is espied from Town Bridge; off the tourist trail is the unspectacular strength and comely charm of Dun Aqueduct.

The wrought Iron Boat, the Swallow, … went at two intervals 1560 yards in four minutes, and 836 yards in two minutes and twenty-eight seconds. At these high velocities no injury was done to the banks of the canal, but they were not a matter of experiment than such as are ever intended to be kept up in a regular trade, which will not exceed eight or nine miles per hour.

Though the so-called 'Scotch' boat was designed to carry goods and/or passengers, it was the latter trade that became its forte. With upwards of 40 passengers being carried each way between Bradford and Bath in less than 90 minutes it was not long before there were two (horse-drawn) trips daily with first and second class accommodation in the long cabin as well as musical entertainment.

Such craft could only operate in lightly-locked or lock-free sections of the navigation. Though there were passenger-carrying operations at the eastern end, it was on the two lock-free pounds – the Long Pound between Devizes and Wootton Rivers and the Nine-mile Pound between Bath and Bradford – that such enterprises flourished. A GWR-authorised speed restriction of 4mph not surprisingly put paid to such operations and helped further their own passenger-carrying trade.

Despite their virtual monopoly of the passenger-carrying market, the GWR did not "deem it expedient to encourage the use of Pleasure Boats on the Navigation". One such steam-boat enterprise at Devizes was reluctantly sanctioned in 1859 provided that no parcels or goods were carried. In 1888 William Black's *The Strange Adventures of a House-Boat* was published wherein the *Nameless Barge* traversed the Kennet & Avon from Bristol to Reading. Fiction it may have been but Black clearly had first-hand experience of the navigation as evidenced by his hero's acclamation of the Limpley Stoke Valley, "then we came to Dundas Aqueduct … and here the spacious view was more extensive than ever – the landscape disappearing into tender distances of rose-grey and lightest green, until, at the far horizon line, and melting into the silvery sky, there were touches of pale translucent blue." Pleasure turned to frustration between Hungerford and Newbury, "nor was there any want of exercise for those so inclined; for this Kennet & Avon Canal seems to have quite fallen out of use; and not only had we to open the locks and swing bridges for ourselves, but these had grown so stiff that it was with the greatest toil and difficulty that we got through." So much for the Victorian spirit of adventure!

Nevertheless, Black's fictional travellers are given contemporary credence with the conversion by Robbins & Co. of Honey Street, of a narrowboat into a house-boat which, as *Lucy*, carried her new owner, Charles Penruddocke, through several adventures on the K&A and onto the pages of *The Cosmopolitan* magazine. With long-distance passenger-carrying all but non-existent, save for the unofficial 'lifts' that some cargo-carrying crews indulged in, and pleasure boating in its infancy, the 'outing' was the inevitable compromise. There was never any shortage of excuses for such occasions – Sunday School treats, Royal anniversaries and coronations and public holidays were obvious candidates.

During the First World War, the Red Cross, wise to the recuperative powers of the canal between Avoncliff and Bradford-on-Avon, took the wounded inmates of their nearby Old Court hospital for canal trips in the narrowboat *Bittern*.

Between the wars the navigation's condition had deteriorated to such an extent that the Carr-Ellison family had to rely on the assistance of GWR staff to ensure that their narrow-beam steam launch, *Thetis*, made it through some of the locks. Their 1931 trip through the canal followed hot on the heels of a similar attempt at putting the 'pleasure' into boating by C.H. Smith, whose adventures aboard his small motor launch were published at the time. At the

Truncated but triumphant, Crofton Pumping Station flaunts the strength of its brick while the stonework of Ladies Bridge, delicate and bramble-clad, echoes with the silent memory of a Lady's whim.

This mirrored simplicity of wood and stone is but one of 29 such images at Devizes but the classical curves of Dundas Aqueduct have no equal.

Montague and Ann Lloyd clearly grasped the politics of their 1946 journey from Reading to Bristol in their observation that the GWR were "quite determined that we should reach Bristol, and presumably they were treating us as an experiment to prove that the Canal was navigable, thereby justifying their State grant for its upkeep, and they certainly played the game magnificently and regardless of cost". The cost to the Lloyds was £5 16s for a permit and 2s 6d deposit for a 'winch handle', the latter refundable on production of the said windlass at Hanham. Two years later, the Earl of Lucan (father to the 'missing' Lord) made the same trip in his full-length narrowboat *Hesperus*. One of his crew, ex-Kennet & Avon boatman George Day, recorded his impressions in verse:

> *… Stanton St Bernard soon was passed,*
> *The weed and mud soon held us fast,*
> *For thirteen hours on tackle heaved*
> *Twas nine pm before we're freed …*

The nationalisation of the railways and the subsequent transfer of the canal to control by the Railway Executive (later the Docks & Inland Waterways Executive and, from 1955, British

beginning of the war, Tom and Angela Rolt made their way from Banbury in Oxfordshire to Hungerford (the nearest point on the canal to Aldbourne where Tom had acquired work) in their narrowboat home, *Cressy*, and found the Kennet & Avon to be "the most difficult part of our long journey, a waterway disused and virtually derelict". For Tom Rolt, whose earlier boating experiences are embodied in his classic *Narrow Boat*, this was his first taste of the K&A, an encounter that led him to observe that it "might have been deliberately laid out to create the maximum difficulty for the navigator".

Whatever the correlation between the decay and the impending closure of the Kennet & Avon in particular and the increasing concern for Britain's canals and rivers in general that expressed itself in the foundation of the Inland Waterways Association in 1946, the post-war years saw an increasing number of pleasure boaters trying no less hard than John Gould and John Knill (though admittedly their livelihoods were not at stake) to keep the canal open, to see the promise of their navigation permit fulfilled.

Transport Waterways) made little difference to the authorities' enthusiasm for maintaining the canal as a navigable artery. It was not wholly unexpected therefore that, on 31st May 1950, through-traffic was effectively severed by a stoppage between Newbury and Woolhampton. Both John Gould's and John Knill's trades were immediately thwarted, though at least three pleasure boats were allowed to circumvent the 8-mile 'obstruction'. *Bykenholte* made it to the first ever IWA Festival of Boats (the fore-runner of the annual National Rally) at Market Harborough in August 1950; *Callisto* left the canal in February 1951 while *Dolly Vardon* was, seemingly, the last to make a through passage in the summer of 1951, albeit with the aid of a 'lift' between Newbury and Woolhampton to pass the impassable.

It is not altogether surprising that the last through passage should have been made by a pleasure craft. Trade on, and maintenance to, the canal declined almost hand in hand and what carrying remained was largely localised, though that in itself was not unusual. Few craft ever worked from Bristol to Reading or vice-versa on a regular basis; indeed one of the most successful operations only took in the 9½ miles of the canal between Dundas and Semington. On the other hand, during the late 40s, sea-going yachts were using the waterway between London and Wales in preference to the longer and more hazardous sea voyage round Cornwall.

Almost by definition the pleasure boater wants to experience most, if not all, of a waterway and, though it may not have been a dominant factor at the time, an awareness of this has increasingly given impetus to, and generated support for, rescuing the Kennet & Avon from the ravages of neglect and decay. As the proprietors of the *Sierra Line* discovered between 1950 and 1951, passenger-carrying *is* trade and though this embryonic boat-hire business based at Honey Street may seem rather Heath Robinson-ish today, it suffered no less than others from the state of the canal. Perhaps John Gould had a vision of things to come for, during the early 50s, as legal wrangles continued unabated to save the canal from further deterioration, he was running a passenger trip-boat, the *Limpley Stoke*, at Newbury; coincidentally the 70s saw John Knill doing much the same at Bathampton.

The 'statistics' of the first volleys in the fight to save the Kennet & Avon, the formation of the Kennet & Avon Canal Trust and the subsequent restoration of the navigation, are detailed elsewhere. Suffice to say here that it has been a long and hard-fought struggle that saw through-navigation in August 1990. Setting aside the high points and the set-backs, there remains the vision and determination of those within – and without – the K&ACT who made the 'psychological leap' and saw restoration neither in terms of a return to what was nor as a narrow local phenomenon but rather as a unique opportunity to realise the amenity potential of an unrivalled and diverse legacy.

In March 1803, while Charles Dundas, Chairman of the K&ACC, and his Committee were considering a letter from John Rennie bemoaning the quality of the stone being used 'in the Works' and advocating the future use of brick, his

Via the restored Claverton Pumping Station, the timeless waters of the Avon feed the canal above ... and the voracious appetite of the dank depths of Bath Deep Lock, Planning Man's endearingly grotesque solution to a problem of his own making.

Netham's canal-like setting, elegant and functional, is but a stone's throw from Bristol's Floating Harbour, a unique inner-city waterscape where tall masts have all but given way to tillers and the paraphernalia of leisure and pleasure.

namesake, Lord Dundas, Governor of the Forth & Clyde Canal Company, was supervising an unusual experiment on his canal. The windswept conditions on the Forth & Clyde were ideal for William Symington's latest brainchild, the steam-powered tug, *Charlotte Dundas*, to be put to the test; in just six hours his unique craft had towed two sloops the 19½ miles to Glasgow, its steam-powered paddle-wheel battling against a strong headwind straight into the history books.

During the early 1960s, through the inventive inspiration of Cecil Wray-Bliss, an erstwhile pontoon, fitted with a 30hp diesel engine and hydraulically-operated central side-paddles and emblazoned with the name *Charlotte Dundas*, gave countless weekend visitors to the canal their first real taste of the Kennet & Avon between Bath and Bathampton. She moved on to Devizes to be run by the Trust, thence into private hands while, for a time, a more modern *Charlotte Dundas* plied the same Long Pound waters. Though 'Wray's' boat was neither *the* first nor *his* first, it was, no less than Symington's, a landmark, not least in the numerous Trust and private trip-boats it spawned. Such operations have always had two allies: that people enjoy being by and on the water, and that, unwittingly, John Hore and John Rennie and their paymasters created for posterity a commercial artery which, while abundant in the artefacts and architecture of its youth, is unrivalled in the diversity and richness of its scenic setting.

The 1990s saw the realisation of many dreams. Through navigation was a reality by August 1990, albeit within the ever-present strictures of water provision. This, in turn, was improved six years later with the commissioning of back pumping at the Devizes flight. However, detailed surveys pointed to more long-term problems which, in turn, led to a bid to The Heritage Lottery Fund. In November 1996, the bid was granted and there began a six-year programme to secure the future of the waterway, its structure, operation and environment.

Almost 200 years after the opening of the Kennet & Avon Canal, the waterway is once again a thriving artery and, more importantly, has a future secured by rather than threatened by newer technologies. Today, more than at any other time, to walk beside or cruise along any part of the Kennet & Avon is not only to absorb its past and share in its present but is also, and above all else, to touch its future, to proclaim, as did the crew of the *Nameless Barge*, that the splendour of the Kennet & Avon is no fiction:

The red kine hardly moved in the meadows golden with buttercups. The olive-green masses of the elms, rising far into the pale blue of the heavens, did not stir a leaf. The warm sunlight seemed to draw forth a hundred scents from the herbs and flowers, that hung in the motionless air. And as if all those glowing colours of bush and tree and blossom were not in themselves enough, we had them repeated on the mirror-like surface of the canal – an inverted fairy-land, with the various hues and tints mysteriously softened and blended together.

opposite: Kelston Mill's redundant annealing ovens at one with today's river traffic around Saltford Lock

Map Key

Each map is broadly similar in format. In addition to the map itself, there are six main areas of text, lettered A, B, C, D, E and F on the facsimile below. The layout of some pages has been slightly altered to facilitate the changing line of the navigation and to maintain the north-south orientation parallel to the book's spine.

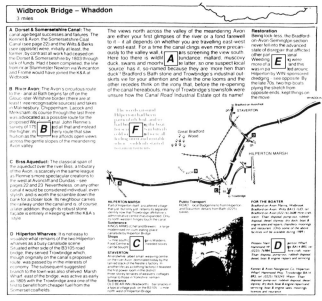

A The General Introduction to each map sets the scene and being in general terms has no specific east-west or west-east bias.

B Points of Special Interest unfold alphabetically and relate to particular features or aspects of the navigation likewise labelled on the map. They are in west-east order but, of course, are easily assimilated in reverse order.

C Information on Towns and Villages includes a brief description as well as details of sustenance, shops, sightseeing and public transport where applicable. General shopping facilities are indicated on the map as are remote or sporadic facilities; neither is mentioned in the text unless there is some unusual or special factor involved. Bristol, Bath, Bradford-on-Avon, Devizes, Newbury and Reading are featured separately on pages 18, 19, 28, 29, 44 and 45 respectively.

D For the Boater gives details of the boater-orientated facilities as well as relevant navigation information and advice and is coloured blue, as is similar information on the map.

E The Restoration of the Kennet & Avon is detailed here in terms of both when a particular stretch or lock flight fell into disuse and how and when it was restored and became navigable.

For the Walker replaces the *Restoration* section on six maps where restoration of the navigation was not a factor. Co-incidentally it is on those stretches that the towpath deviates from its normal navigation-side route; alternatives for the walker are thus detailed here.

opposite: Boaters enjoy a day out at Bradford-on-Avon

F Extracts from Through England's Waterways are included alongside alternate maps. Written in the late 40s by Montague and Ann Lloyd, the book embodies much of the flavour of the embryonic days of pleasure-boating on the Kennet & Avon.

In addition each map is headed with details of its parameters, including the number of miles, locks and swing-bridges, as well as a linear map of the whole navigation on which the map's exact location is indicated by an arrow.

Boaters can project relevant cruising times (in hours or fractions thereof) by adding together the number of miles, locks and swing-bridges and dividing the total by 4. Clearly heavily-locked sections (such as Devizes) or lock-free stretches (such as the Long Pound) will tend to upset the theory!

All addresses and telephone numbers were correct in May 1999.

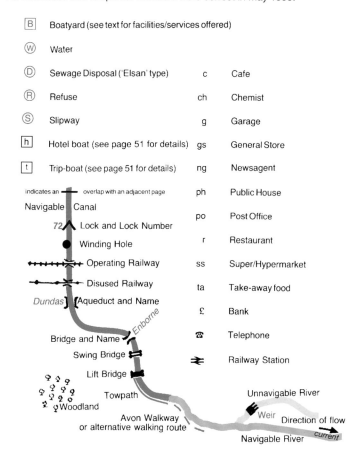

B	Boatyard (see text for facilities/services offered)		
W	Water		
D	Sewage Disposal ('Elsan' type)	c	Cafe
R	Refuse	ch	Chemist
S	Slipway	g	Garage
h	Hotel boat (see page 51 for details)	gs	General Store
t	Trip-boat (see page 51 for details)	ng	Newsagent
	indicates an overlap with an adjacent page	ph	Public House
	Navigable Canal	po	Post Office
72	Lock and Lock Number	r	Restaurant
	Winding Hole	ss	Super/Hypermarket
	Operating Railway	ta	Take-away food
	Disused Railway	£	Bank
Dundas	Aqueduct and Name	☎	Telephone
	Bridge and Name		Railway Station
	Swing Bridge		
	Lift Bridge		
	Towpath		Unnavigable River
	Woodland		Weir · Direction of flow
	Avon Walkway or alternative walking route		Navigable River · current

Note that no turning points are indicated on the River Avon as it is possible to turn even the longest craft on most stretches

Clifton Suspension Bridge – Feeder Canal
3½ miles • 1 lock

A Clifton Suspension Bridge: In 1829 Isambard Kingdom Brunel won the competition to design a bridge worthy of spanning the rocky chasm of the Avon Gorge at fashionable Clifton. However, it was not until 1864, five years after Brunel's death, that his dramatic design finally united both sides of the gorge. Brunel's vision, though ultimately modified through financial considerations, was chosen in preference to a more mundane concept from the celebrated canal and road engineer, Thomas Telford, and the 'single immense arch of stone … (with) immense abutments carrying twenty dwelling houses, a lighthouse, toll house, chapel, granaries, a water mill, cotton and wool factories, a marine school, a library, a museum…', brainchild, not of Heath Robinson, but of a certain Mr Bridge!

B Floating Harbour and New Cut: The curiously-named Floating Harbour has its origins back in the growing inadequacies of Bristol as an inland port during the 18th century. William Jessop it was who largely designed 'the Float', as it was often known, and the works were completed in 1809 – coincidentally the year before the rivers Kennet and Avon were finally linked. Jessop's legacy is a deep-water dock which generally corresponds to the original course of the Avon, a new course for which was cut to the south between Rownham in the west and Totterdown in the east.

C St Augustine's Reach: Bristol's most central and best-known waterside, St Augustine's Reach, dates back to the 13th century when the river Frome was diverted from its natural junction with the Avon by Bristol Bridge. For 1248 it was spectacular engineering and established Bristol as a major port rather than the (then) nearby rival hamlet of Redcliffe.

D Totterdown: What today is no more than a sharp bend in the channel was conceived as a sort of waterways crossroads. Here the New Cut rejoined the natural course of the Avon, the Feeder Canal being cut, not only to maintain the navigation to Bath (by-passing Netham Weir), but also to ensure a direct flow of fresh water through the Floating Harbour. The lock that once formed the 'crossroads' has long since gone.

Whether your first taste of Bristol's Floating Harbour follows the spectacular rigours of the Avon Gorge or (more likely) the decaying industrial backdrop and embryonic offices between Totterdown and Bristol Bridge, the end result is the same – a fascinating and unique waterfront world where sea-going motor yachts, river cruisers and narrowboats rub gunwales. From water and quayside alike the Floating Harbour exudes history, nostalgia and charm; it is an unparalleled amenity that Bristol nearly lost but which, since the 1980s, has contributed much to the city's pride in itself. If you're on the water tie up and take to Shanks's pony; if you're already afoot explore the water awhile at your leisure aboard one of the bright yellow ferries … and whatever your mode of travel the walk on page 58 is a must!

For the Walker
The absence of a towpath between Bristol Bridge and Netham Lock forces the walker to venture 'inland'. The recommended Avon Walkway route is marked on the map and has the advantage of taking in part of the non-navigable Avon east of Totterdown. That said, several alternative road routes offer a variety of inner-city scenery.

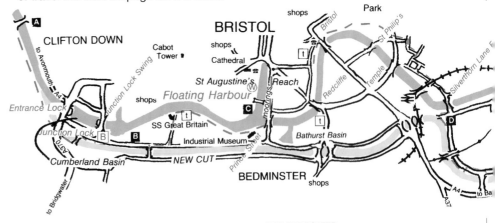

BRISTOL FLOATING HARBOUR
Detailed information on Bristol can be found on page 18; the following relates only to the waterfront area close to the Floating Harbour's only 'temporary' moorings along Narrow Quay.

Sustenance
ARNOLFINI – a former tea warehouse (Bush House) but now a contemporary arts complex that includes bar and restaurant with excellent, and unusual, snacks.
WATERFRONT TAVERN – large inn with hot and cold food – seafood a speciality; waterside just north of the Arnolfini.
THE BRASSHOUSE – a large, bright pub with wide range of food in erstwhile sheds on east-facing side of St Augustine's Reach.
WATERSHED – bar and restaurants form part of a modern media centre based in what was E shed, waterside just north of the Brasshouse.

Shops
There are few 'basics' shops around the waterfront; Bristol's main shopping area is a short walk north and east from Neptune's statue and/or north-west from Bristol Bridge.

Sightseeing
FLOATING HARBOUR – this is one large 'attraction' in itself and features in the walk described on page 58.

Public Transport
WATER – regular ferry services criss-cross the Harbour; details from Bristol (0117) 9275 3416.

FOR THE BOATER
Boats with an air-draught of over 6ft 6in may need to have Prince Street Bridge swung – 'phone the Bridge Operator on Bristol (0117) 929 9338 to arrange this (Apr-Sept, 0600-2230; Oct-Mar, 0900-1645)

The speed limit in the Floating Harbour is 6mph.

Craft should sound one prolonged horn blast before passing under Prince Street, Redcliffe and Bristol Bridges. Two-way navigation applies through all bridgeways except Temple Meads Railway Arches where craft should always keep to the starboard (right-hand) of the two arches.

All boaters are advised to obtain a copy of Bristol Harbour's *Information for Boat Owners* – see page 51.

Temporary pleasure-craft moorings at Narrow Quay are marked on the map.

Craft should approach the sharp bend at Totterdown with caution and sound a prolonged blast as a warning to approaching craft.

Anglo-Welsh Waterway Holidays, Avon Quay, Cumberland Basin, Bristol BS1 6XL; tel: Bristol (0117) 924 1200. Narrowboat hire, day-boat hire, water, gas, diesel, pump-out, rubbish disposal, boat repairs, K&A windlasses.

The river approach to (or departure from) Bristol is one of scenic and sensory contrasts: from the overhanging, almost primeval, vegetation of Fox's Wood to the razed industrial remnants of Crew's Hole; from the impatient surge of trains in and out of St Anne's Tunnel to the tranquil pace of the local rowing club; from the grandeur of Hencliff Wood to the man-made directness of the Feeder Canal. It is a time for re-adjustment, an opportunity to come to terms with the new order of things … to understand that the scenic attributes of man-made cuts are accidents of time while the river's time-worn course flaunts its basic affinity with nature's whims. Here, perhaps more than any other part of the navigable Avon, the river has reclaimed, almost unscathed, the privacy of its valley.

For the Walker
Walking between Bath and Bristol is for the most part straight-forward – the original river towpath, the Avon Walkway and the Cycleway (the old Midland Railway track bed) making up most of the route. There is, however, no direct waterside path between the Floating Harbour and Netham Lock, the Avon Walkway route via the New Cut being recommended.

> "Reaching Hanham Lock … and leaving the Kennet & Avon Canal, we regretfully handed over our handle and canal pass to the lock-keeper and proceeded down the River Avon under the ideal conditions of a beautiful wide river with no weed trouble and even with other pleasure boats adding gaiety to the scene."

A Feeder Canal: The almost straight mile of the Feeder Canal by-passes a meandering stretch of natural river to the south and east. It is not a pretty place; old and newer industries in various stages of apathy line one side while incessant traffic rattles along the Feeder Road on the other. Nevertheless it is this cut that ensures passage to and from Bath and at the same time alleviates the problem of water stagnation in the Floating Harbour. Originally it brought with it its own form of 'stagnation' for, as the Bristol Mercury recorded in the 1880s, it was "the chosen home of the manure manufacturers, bone-crushing mills, knacker yards, horse flesh-boiling factories … causing stench-laden folds of air to envelope [sic] the visitor …"

B Netham Lock: The bay just south and east of Netham Lock is all that remains of the Feeder Cut, a short channel, complete with lock, that by-passed Netham Dam while the Feeder Canal was being constructed. Netham Lock and its attendant lock-keeper's cottage could be almost anywhere on the inland waterways network, yet this microcosm of canalia links a busy urban waterway with a tidal river.

C Crew's Hole: The erstwhile industrial complex known as Crew's Hole (on some maps 'Screw's Hole') has been terminally eradicated by 20th-century Planning Man. The swish riverside housing belies the fact that 'stench-laden folds of air' were once the norm hereabouts with the river an open sewer carrying the unwanted seaward. One of the last industries to flourish (if that's the right word) was a tar distillery originally built to meet Brunel's needs for creosote as a preservative for railway sleepers. Almost all has gone … but the lone chimney atop Trooper's Hill, built to expel the collective toxicity of the vale below, remains as both a monument and a sentinel.

D Hanham Colliery Wharf: Amid the bosky splendour of Fox's and Hencliff Woods is the partially overgrown wharf that once dispatched coal by river from Hanham Colliery above. Piercing the trees is the mine's attendant slag heap, like the wharf, an overgrown memorial of sorts.

Netham Lock/Toll Office
FEEDER CANAL
Netham Acrow Panel
current
weir
ST ANNE'S
Pinney Terrace
ST PHILIP'S MARSH
NEW CUT
BROOM HILL
shops
Tunnel
Conham Vale
RIVER AVON
Hencliff Wood
Fox's Wood
Jurisdiction
Port of Bristol | British Waterways
HANHAM MILLS
tidal

FOR THE BOATER
Navigation through Netham Lock (both sets of gates are usually open) is possible during normal working hours (longer Apr–Sept) – river conditions per-mitting. Phone Bristol (0117) 977 6590 for opening hours and cruising conditions.

The Avon is tidal downstream of Hanham Lock; extreme caution should be exercised at times of heavy rainfall and/or spring tides. If in doubt contact either the Netham lock-keeper on Bristol (0117) 977 6590 or Hanham Lock on Bristol (0117) 986 2550 for up-to-date information.

All craft on the Avon should carry an anchor.

Always moor facing upstream when stopping for a prolonged period.

Don't moor on the river when in flood or during spring tides.

Netham Lock-keeper's Office, Netham Lock, Netham Road, Bristol BS5 9PQ; tel: Bristol (0117) 977 6590. Short-term permits for navigating and mooring in the Floating Harbour available.

ST PHILIP'S MARSH (BRISTOL)
This is the area of Bristol that includes Feeder Road which runs alongside the Feeder Canal; there are a few shops at the Totterdown end but mooring here is not recommended.

BROOM HILL (BRISTOL)
The area of Bristol atop St Anne's Railway Tunnel.

Sustenance
BEESE'S TEA GARDENS – founded in 1846, this offers the only accessible refreshment (fully licensed) between Bristol and Hanham Lock. There is good mooring but, if this be occupied at weekends (between April and September), tie up on the towpath and call across for the ferry. Parties catered for – book in advance (0117) 977 7412

Shops
The 'basics' are available on the main road above Beese's; the proprietors are happy for boaters and walkers to take advantage of these … having first supped with them, of course.

Public Transport
ROAD – City bus service details from Bristol (0117) 955 3231.

Hanham Mills – Bitton
4 miles • 2 locks

A Hanham Lock: One hundred yards downstream of Hanham Lock an imaginary line divides the river between British Waterways' jurisdiction and that of Bristol City Council – formerly the Port of Bristol. Hanham Lock is numbered '1', officially the first on the Kennet & Avon Canal. That said, Hanham, like all the river locks between Bristol and Bath, started life as part of the Avon Navigation which opened in 1727 and saw considerable trade of Shropshire coal up-river and Bath stone down-river. Should you perchance espy a stoat-like snout peering out from the island between weir and lock, it is but one of a colony of mink for which this is home ... home, that is, until the river starts to rise when, with instinctive foresight, they abandon their island to take refuge on the higher ground by the lock-keeper's house.

B Somerdale Chocolate Factory: Cadbury-Schweppes' (originally Fry's) Chocolate Factory dominates the navigation from both east and west of its Somerdale site. It has been described as a "red-brick monster" but if the alternative is concrete and plastic then the 'monster' becomes as acceptable as the seductive odours it exudes. The factory was originally part of a 1920s 'garden factory' concept, with its workforce at one with the beauty of their surroundings and the sweetness of their product.

C Avon & Gloucestershire Railway: The A&GR was literally and financially an appendage of the Kennet & Avon Canal Company. Its two river wharves, either side of Keynsham Lock – Avon and Londonderry – provided tramroad links with south Gloucestershire's Coalpit Heath collieries from 1832. Both tramroads predated the age of steam and, like the navigation itself, ultimately became a victim of it; even the Midland Railway's attempt to incorporate part of the track into its Bath branch failed, although the line to Avon Wharf was to enjoy a revival between 1881 and 1904. The lines of both tramroads are traceable up the hillside.

D Avon Mill: Since the flood-prevention schemes of the 1970s, the few remaining relics of what was one of the river's oldest and most substantial brass mills, Keynsham's Avon Mill, are no longer by the water. A short walk town-wards will reveal all there is.

To all intents and purposes the river above Hanham Lock (1) is not influenced by the tidal flow that begins its surge upstream 14 miles away at Avonmouth. Nevertheless there is a lot of fresh water around between Hanham and Bitton as no less than five tributaries of the Avon join it in a little over three miles. Travelling east-west these are the River Boyd, Broadmead Brook, Warmley (or Siston) Brook, the River Chew and Scotland Brook. Only the River Chew keeps its confluence to itself ... unless, that is, the intrepid traveller ventures accidentally down Keynsham's weir stream to view what little remains of one of the most prestigious brass mills on the river. When you've finished playing 'spot-the-river' keep a weather nose open for Fry's Chocolate Factory and speculate instead on what that flavour-ful aroma might be.

HANHAM MILLS

weir
ph
Cleeve Wood
Park Corner
tidal
current
non-tidal
C
Londonderry Wharf
B
to Bristol
2
ph
County
White Hart
ph
current
B
B
weir
D
A4
KEYNSHAM
shops
Avon Wharf
RIVER AVON
shops
BITTON ph
A431 to Bath
Cycleway
Bitton Railway Path

For the Walker
For the most part the Avon Walkway uses the river towpath though officially it doubles up with the Cycleway and takes a short cut across the loop of river that includes Swineford and Saltford Locks (3 & 4). It is possible to get closer to both locks by continuing along the towpath, the A431, more towpath and doubling back across the river on the Cycleway (see page 17).

"Once our after-rope was left hanging over the stern and was seized upon by the propeller. It took hours to cut it away and cost me my only spare safety razor blade."

HANHAM MILLS
Hanham itself is not easily accessible from the river.
Sustenance
CHEQUERS INN – large out-of-town hostelry with bar food and restaurant; riverside by Hanham Weir.
OLD LOCK & WEIR – small pub with bar snacks and live music; riverside by Hanham Weir.

KEYNSHAM
'Twixt Bristol and Bath, Keynsham town centre is now by-passed by road, its streets but a short walk to the south-west, all the more agreeable because of it.
Sustenance
LOCK-KEEPER – bar food; riverside between County and White Hart Bridges. There are several excellent pubs in the town, the nearest being PIONEER and LONDON INN. Non-pub eating-out at the OLD MANOR HOUSE HOTEL, tel: Bristol (0117) 986 3107.
Shops
All the usual facilities, including banks.

Sightseeing
KEYNSHAM ABBEY – a few remains of the 12th-century Abbey survive in Abbey Park.
Public Transport
RAIL – regular service to Bristol and Bath; details from 0345 484950.

BITTON
This main-road village is most easily reached via the old Midland Railway – mooring is possible against its northern pier. Now repopulated after the 18th-century activities of the Cock Road Gang – one judge felt he had "hanged the whole of that parish".
Sustenance
WHITE HART – roadside hostelry with restaurant.
Sightseeing
BITTON STATION – static railway displays every weekend; trips 'in steam' every Sunday, Mar-Nov; details from Bitton (0117) 932 7296; easy access of Cycleway, a mile north-west of the river.
Public Transport
ROAD – regular Badgerline services to Keynsham and Bitton from Bath and Bristol; details from Bath (01225) 464446.

FOR THE BOATER
The Avon is tidal downstream of Hanham Lock. In flood or high tide conditions seek and listen to the advice of the Hanham keeper – tel: Bristol (0117) 986 2550. Keynsham Lock cut is not immediately obvious when cruising downstream; be prepared for a sharp right-hand turn and for craft leaving Portavon Marina; a horn blast would give warning of your approach.

Boaters navigating the K&A will require a special windlass.

BW Hanham Lock/Toll Office; tel: Bristol (0117) 986 2550. Short-term BW and Bristol Docks licences available; also K&A windlasses and BW keys.

Portavon Marina, Bitton Road, Keynsham BS31 2TD; tel: Bristol (0117) 986 1626. Water, 'Elsan' disposal, rubbish disposal, gas, diesel, slipway, cranage, boat & engine repairs & sales, chandlery, toilets, brokerage, winter storage, K&A windlasses and BW licences.

Phoenix Marine, Unit 12a, Broadmead Lane, Keynsham; tel: Bristol (0117) 986 4181. Boat-building, moorings.

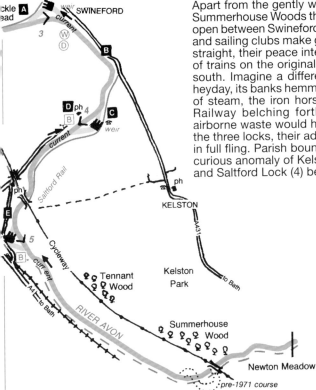

Apart from the gently wooded slopes of Tennant and Summerhouse Woods the river valley is generally more open between Swineford and Newbridge. Local rowing and sailing clubs make good use of the so-called mile straight, their peace interrupted by the periodic rattle of trains on the original GWR Bath-Bristol line to the south. Imagine a different scene in the Navigation's heyday, its banks hemmed in by two boisterous heads of steam, the iron horses of the GWR and Midland Railway belching forth alongside. Less dramatic airborne waste would have been a feature at each of the three locks, their adjacent copper and brass mills in full fling. Parish boundaries are responsible for the curious anomaly of Kelston Lock (5) being in Saltford and Saltford Lock (4) being in Kelston.

For the Walker

The most direct route between Bath's outskirts and the Bitton-Swineford area is via the Avon Walkway and the Cycleway, joining or leaving the latter at Mead Road, Saltford. To take in the river loop denied by this route it is necessary to re-cross the river (between the old towpath and the Walkway) via the Cycleway – see map.

A Swineford Mill:
The mill buildings at Swineford started and finished life in the cloth industry, first as a tucking mill and then as a flock mill. But in its heyday, between 1709 and 1859, it was a vibrant outpost of Bristol's brass and copper industry, indeed it was the last of the river's many mills to cease production.

B Golden Valley Wharf:
This small, and today picturesque wharf was so-named after the Golden Valley Mill on the river Boyd at Bitton. Although originally a brass mill, the wharf's associations are solely with the mill's paper manufacture which began in 1825 and continued into this century.

C Kelston Mill:
Originally a 'copper forge and brass manufactory', Kelston Mill ended its associations with the industry in the late 1840s as a battery mill (the process of extending and shaping metal by beating with a hammer). Its two unlined annealing ovens and adjacent buildings have recently been restored.

D Saltford Lock and the *Jolly Sailor:*
The Avon Navigation opened in 1727 amid conflicts fired by rival interests. Both Somerset and Kingswood colliers, for example, saw the enterprise solely in terms of the Shropshire coal now available to the area with which their own coal, which relied on poor and costly road transport, could not compete. It was such rivalries that, in 1738, inspired "Persons unknown" to destroy Saltford Lock and to threaten further action "unless an immediate Stop was put to the sending of any coals by water". The coal did get through and some, no doubt, was used to keep the adjacent *Jolly Sailor* – originally the mill house to a leather mill – warm. The inn's fireplace has strong connections with the navigation, it having been the custom that a newly-promoted barge captain should thrust a red-hot poker into the fireplace's wooden surround before buying his crew a round. The holes remain to this day.

E Saltford's Old Brass Mill:
Formerly a fulling mill, the mill downstream of Kelston Lock became part of the brass industry by 1721 and in 1908 was still working as a brass battery mill, the last in the country to do so. The rolling of sheet brass continued here until 1925.

FOR THE BOATER
Boaters should not tie up in Saltford Lock (4) to avail themselves of *The Jolly Sailor.*

Watch out for sailing dinghies between Saltford and Kelston Locks (4 & 5) and remember that power gives way to sail.

Do not moor by the Sailing Club's slipway above Saltford Lock.

Bristol Boats, Sheppard's Boatyard, Mead Lane, Saltford; tel: Bath (01225) 872032. Water, gas, slipway, moorings, trailable boat sales, outboard engine sales and repairs, chandlery.

Saltford Marina, The Shallows, Saltford; tel: Bath (01225) 872226. Water, 'Elsan' disposal, pump-out, rubbish disposal, gas, slipway, craneage, hard standing, undercover servicing, boat & engine repairs, boat sales & brokerage, marine finance, permanent & temporary moorings, toilets, shower & laundry facilities, 24-hr security, Riverside Restaurant (tel: Bath (01225) 873862).

SWINEFORD
The name derives from the legend of Bladud who, when the pigs he was tending caught his leprosy, escaped the pending wrath of his employer by shepherding them across the river here – hence 'swine-ford'. The pigs made it to Bath, fell into a morass that cured their ailment and invented Bath Spa. Possible mooring places down- and up-stream of Swineford Weir; 'round-the-loop' walkers will come this way anyway.
Sustenance
SWAN – bar food; on the main A431.

SALTFORD
In recent years the village has spread across the main A4 but its origins are closer to the river. It was, reputedly, at the Old Brass Mill that Handel first heard the 'battering' of brass which in turn inspired his 'Hallelujah Chorus'.
Sustenance
JOLLY SAILOR – bar food and a surfeit of riverside lore; backs onto Saltford Lock.
BIRD IN HAND – bar snacks and strong

railway connections; ½ mile south-west of Saltford Lock (4).
Sightseeing
SALTFORD CHURCH – the porch boasts a gravestone that tells the story of Francis Flood whose legs are buried here! The adjoining manor house is one of Britain's oldest inhabited dwellings.
Public Transport
ROAD – regular Badgerline service to/ from Swineford and Saltford to Bath and Bristol; details from Bath (01225) 464446.

BRISTOL

Early photographs of Bristol depict a vibrant 19th-century city. Tall masts line busy quay walls, narrow streets and alleys filter down to broader thoroughfares, nameplates and signs hang out over multifarious frontages … while bustling handcarts, bicycles and people are momentarily frozen in the camera's curious eye. Paradoxically it is a picture of Bristol in decline for the city's so-called 'Golden Age' had seen its sun finally set with the abolition of slavery in the 1830s.

A century and a half on, Bristol has come to terms with its past and its decline; perhaps it can even be thankful that northern rivals such as Birmingham, Manchester and Liverpool, protégés of the Industrial Revolution, usurped its position as a second in the kingdom and the capital's western counterpart.

Bricg-stowe, 'the place of the bridge', has its origins in the high neck of land between the confluence of the rivers Avon and Frome. It was the 13th-century diversion of the latter that gave Bristol its supremacy over rival centres of habitation, such as Redcliffe, and laid the basis for its maritime potential, an asset it fully exploited when its western location came into its own as the natural springboard for exploration of the Americas.

John Cabot's pre-Columbus expedition from Bristol, which led to the 'discovery' of Newfoundland, is well-documented; more difficult to substantiate is the theory that the Americas were so-called after the Port of Bristol's Collector of Customs at the time, Richard Amerycke. Fact or fiction, the plethora of such sea-faring yarns typifies a city that has re-discovered itself.

A new and vibrant Bristol has emerged from the disillusionment of decline and the battering of the Blitz, a city eager to flaunt its extraordinary heritage and in particular its Floating Harbour which, though it came too late to re-establish Bristol's economic fortunes and status, is proving to be today's outstanding asset.

Shopping
Almost all the usual 'High Street' stores are represented in the city. In general terms the Broadmead shopping area caters more for the 'basics' while the Park Street area has more 'specialist' shops. Among other things the Corn Market near Bristol Bridge offers a wide range of fruit and vegetable stores.

Sustenance
As would be expected of a large city, the choice is as diverse as it is endless. On the whole the following pubs and restaurants are located within a few hundred yards of the Floating Harbour but that is not to say that the choice is any less varied 'beyond the pale'.

Pubs
LLANDOGER TROW – modern food in the olde worlde surroundings of King Street.
THE OLD DUKE – beer, pub grub and jazz in King Street.
THE COTTAGE – good food and large helpings waterside just west of SS Great Britain.
PLUME OF FEATHERS – small and intimate local with bar snacks on the Hotwell Road (behind the Sand Dock).
PUMPHOUSE – excellent selection of food amid the traditional harbour-side surroundings of Cumberland Basin.
NOVA SCOTIA – bar snacks and hot lunches in harbour-side pub steeped in local sea-faring lore.
OSTRICH INN – home-cooked pub grub on the waterfront at Bathurst Basin.

Eating Out
THE GLASS BOAT – superb food afloat including excellent weekday breakfasts alongside Welsh Back by Bristol Bridge.
VINTNER – home-made food and extensive wine list in 16th-century building in St Stephen's Street, north-east of Neptune.
RIVERSTATION – licensed restaurant upstairs, café/deli bar down; special food in special waterfront setting northside between Prince Street and Redcliffe Bridges.
AQUA – excellent French-style bistro on Welsh Back.
HOWARDS – superb and in-all-the-best-guides up-market French and local speciality cuisine served in down-beat surroundings just south of Junction Lock.
CATHAY RENDEZVOUS – fine Chinese cuisine housed in a beautifully restored Georgian Building on King Street.
TRATTORIA DA RENATO – authentic Italian and international cuisine in setting often frequented by 'stars' from the nearby Bristol Old Vic in King Street.

Entertainments
BRISTOL OLD VIC – King Street; tel: Bristol (0117) 987 7877.
BRISTOL HIPPODROME – St Augustine's Parade; tel: (0117) 929 9444.
COLSTON HALL – Colston Street; tel: Bristol (0117) 922 3686.
ARNOLFINi – Narrow Quay; tel: Bristol (0117) 929 9191.
WATERSHED – Canon's Road; tel: Bristol (0117) 925 3845.
ABC CINEMAS – Frogmore Street; tel: Bristol (0117) 926 2849.
ODEON FILM CENTRE – Union Street; tel: Bristol (0117) 929 0882.

Exhibitions/Museums
ARNOLFINI – Narrow Quay; tel: Bristol (0117) 929 9191.
BRISTOL CITY MUSEUM and ART GALLERY – Queen's Road; tel: Bristol (0117) 929 9771.
BRISTOL INDUSTRIAL MUSEUM – Prince's Wharf; tel: Bristol (0117) 29 9771
WATERSHED – Canon's Road; tel: Bristol (0117) 927 6444.
ST NICHOLAS CHURCH MUSEUM – St Nicholas Street; tel: Bristol (0117) 929 9771; medieval Bristol history and brass rubbings.
SS GREAT BRITAIN & John Cabot's MATTHEW – Great Western Dock, Gas Ferry Road; tel: Bristol (0117) 929 1843
MARITIME HERITAGE CENTRE – Wapping Wharf, Gas Ferry Road; tel: Bristol (0117) 929 1843.
JOHN WESLEY'S THE NEW ROOM – The Horsefair; the world's oldest Methodist Chapel.
BRUNEL ENGINE SHED – Temple Meads Station; tel: Bath (01225) 26393 and Bristol (0117) 929 2688
NATIONAL LIFEBOAT MUSEUM – Prince's Wharf; tel: Bristol (0117) 921 3389.
HARVEY'S WINE MUSEUM – Denmark Street; tel: Bristol (0117) 927 766
@t BRISTOL – Harbourside; tel: Bristol (0117) 909 2000; hands-on science centre; opens spring 2000.

Sightseeing
FLOATING HARBOUR – a sight in itself; the walk on pages 58 and 59 has all the details.
TEMPLE CHURCH – off Victoria Street; famous for its leaning tower that's been in danger of falling over since 1400.
CORN EXCHANGE – Corn Street; the bronze 'nails' gave rise to the expressing 'paying on the nail'.
BROAD STREET – a mixture of architectural styles including the art nouveau frontage of the former Edward Everard printing house and the church built over the medieval vaulted town wall gateway.
COLLEGE GREEN – two architectural styles vie for attention; Bristol Cathedral, "one of the best cathedral interiors in England" according to John Betjeman, and the sweeping neo-Georgian crescent of the Council House.

Information
TOURIST INFORMATION CENTRE – St Nicholas Church, St Nicholas Street, Bristol, BS1 1UE; tel: (0117) 926 0767.

Public Transport
RAIL – Temple Meads, Temple Gate; tel: 0345 484950
ROAD – Bus Station, Marlborough Street; tel: Bristol (0117) 955 3231.
WATER – Harbour ferries; tel: Bristol (0117) 9927 3416.

BATH

Most potted tours of Britain include a visit to Bath. Drawn by the architectural showpieces of Roman ruins and Georgian grandeur, the visitor's eye is easily seduced by this elegant city's extraordinary heritage.

Bath's earliest settlers (the story of one, Bladud, father to King Lear, is related on page 17) soon realised the potential of their hidden assets – Britain's only hot springs. A spa was born! The Romans exploited the daily 250,000 gallon dose on a much grander scale, dedicating the adjacent temple to the goddess Sulis Minerva, a convenient, though not uncommon, merger of the Celtic Sul with the Roman Minerva, and naming the settlement, Aquae Sulis.

This was the stage set for the emergence of Bath as a focal point of Georgian fashion. The 18th-century 're-discovery' of Roman Bath coincided with the city's rise to prominence as a place of genteel elegance and curative waters. The taste of Beau Nash, the creativity of, among others, John Wood, and the softness of the local Bath stone together begat a unique city.

That said, much of what was Aquae Sulis has yet to be discovered, for under the paved passages with their intimate shops and wine bars lies an ancient world, a world which archaeologist, Barry Cunliffe, would like to see excavated, not at the expense of today's Bath but rather as a subterranean time-trap, a mellow nether-world, rich in images of the Roman occupation.

One day, perhaps, such a dream may be realised; in the meantime, only a few feet above, tourists trample time-worn trails round Circus and Crescent, Abbey and Baths, refurbished stone and reborn spas, innumerable eyes straining to glimpse an ever-elusive magic. Should you get the chance, walk these streets instead in the privacy of the dawn's eastern light and share the reality of this singularly beautiful city with yourself.

Shopping
Almost all the usual High Street shops are represented but look out for the more unusual and exclusive shops that seem to abound; The Corridor is not to be missed. There are two markets; one, mainly food, is part of the Guildhall complex, the other, mainly crafts, is at Green Park Station.

Sustenance
Every choice imaginable: from the traditional pub to the night club, from Macdonald's to Michelin stars, from Chinese to Provençal. The following can only be a taste of what is available; it is however a selection that hopefully includes something for everyone, price, style and location-wise.

Pubs
THE BOATER – good pub grub in an Edwardian-style atmosphere, close to Pulteney Bridge.
CRYSTAL PALACE – good selection of food in two large bars and patio area in Abbey Green.
THE BELL – good basic pub grub and live music in trendy Walcot Street.
THE OLD GREEN TREE – wide range of lunchtime food in small, intimate pub in central Green Street.
SAM WELLER'S – reasonably-priced food in attractive surroundings close to the centre in Upper Borough Walls.

Eating Out
VENDANGE – excellent and competitively-priced food in 'local' atmosphere; in Margaret's Buildings 'twixt The Circus and Royal Crescent.
CAFE IGUANA – Latin American café bar and restaurant; near the theatre in the Seven Dials complex.
THE RAINCHECK – fashionable cocktail bar in stylish surroundings; behind the theatre in Monmouth Street.
RASCALS BISTRO – adventurous cuisine and excellent wine list; a total experience in Pierrepont Place.
CAPETTI'S – affordable, genuine Italian cuisine in the vaulted depths below Argyle Street.
DEMUTHS – quality home-made snacks and excellent value characterise this North Parade Passage vegetarian eatery.
BEAUJOLAIS – almost Gallic setting renowned for its fine French cuisine; just off Queen Square, in Chapel Row.
GREEN PARK BRASSERIE – Erstwhile railway ticket office transformed into intimate, plant-festooned brasserie with good food and occasional jazz; just north of Midland Bridge.

Entertainments
THEATRE ROYAL – Sawclose; tel: Bath (01225) 448844.
ABC CINEMA – Westgate Street; tel: Bath (01225) 461730.
LITTLE THEATRE CINEMA – St Michael's Place; tel: Bath (01225) 466822.
ROBINS CINEMAS – Monmouth Street; tel: Bath (01225) 461506.

Exhibitions/Museums
ROMAN BATHS MUSEUM – Stall Street; tel: Bath (01225) 477784.
MUSEUM OF COSTUME – Assembly Rooms, Bennett Street; tel: Bath (01225) 477784.
NO.1 ROYAL CRESCENT – restored Georgian residence; tel: Bath (01225) 428126.
BATH INDUSTRIAL HERITAGE CENTRE – Camden Works, Julian Road; tel: Bath (01225) 318348.
VICTORIA ART GALLERY – Bridge Street; tel: Bath (01225) 477772
BUILDING OF BATH MUSEUM – The Vineyards; tel: Bath (01225) 333895. Architectural exhibition in Georgian Gothic chapel.
RPS NATIONAL CENTRE OF PHOTOGRAPHY – Milsom Street; tel: Bath (01225) 462841.
MUSEUM OF BOOKBINDING – Manvers Street; tel: Bath (01225) 466000.
HOLBURNE OF MENSTRIE MUSEUM – Great Pulteney Street; tel: Bath (01225) 466669. Old masters and rare silver, porcelain and enamels and a national collection of Gainsboroughs.
POSTAL MUSEUM – 8 Broad Street; tel: Bath (01225) 460333.
WILLIAM HERSCHEL MUSEUM – New King Street; tel: Bath (01225) 336228. Resplendent with artefacts of William Herschel, musician and astronomer.
MUSEUM OF EAST ASIAN ART – 12 Bennett Street; tel: Bath (01225) 464640. Well-displayed, original, private collection.

Sightseeing
BATH ABBEY – 15th-century; built on site of Saxon Abbey where Edgar was crowned King in 973 AD.
ASSEMBLY ROOMS – Fine suite of rooms designed by John Wood in Bennett Street.
PUMP ROOM – Georgian Pump Rooms and Corinthian columns overlooking the Baths; in Abbey Courtyard.
GUILDHALL – 18th-century Banqueting Room complete with chandeliers and portraits; in High Street.
PULTENEY BRIDGE, the CIRCUS and CRESCENTS should not be missed, especially the view from the less-frequented Camden Crescent.

Racing
For details of race meetings (Apr-Oct) tel: Bath (01225) 424609.

Information
TOURIST INFORMATION CENTRE – Abbey Chambers, Abbey Churchyard, Bath BA1 1LY; tel: Bath (01225) 477101.

Public Transport
RAIL – Bath Spa, Manvers Street/Dorchester Street; for train times tel: 0345 484950.
ROAD – Bus Station, Manvers Street; tel: Bath (01225) 464446.

A Newbridge: With the A4 atop, the New Bridge – formerly the boundary of the city of Bath – is a pleasing structure. The single, 100ft span incorporates seven flood arches and two unusual holes through the arch's spandrels.

B Midland Railway: Not for the first time does the line of the erstwhile Midland Railway cross the Avon. Its circuitous Bristol-to-Bath route was never conceived as a single entity but grew instead over some 40 years out of a number of different railway enterprises. The track is no more but the route today forms the main part of the Bristol & Bath Railway Path and Cycle Route, a 15-mile, almost traffic-less link between the two cities. Sadly, at the Bath end the line between Weston Lock and the Green Park Station terminus is no more. Between Bath and Bitton the Cycleway offers walkers a loftier alternative to the Avon Walkway.

C Dolphin Bridge and Dutch Island: Weston Cut is the longest of the river, its canal-like quality emphasised by the scarcely symmetrical Dolphin Bridge and the adjacent *Dolphin Inn*, its front door, in true canal tradition, facing the water. The digging of the cut created an island which became known as Dutch Island, after the owner of the brass mill established on the river side in the early 18th century; parish registers of nearby Twerton also point to a notable Dutch community.

D Bath's Bridges and Broad Quay: Many of the river's bridges are of special interest. The Midland Railway crossed twice between Weston and the city, the most easterly bridge now linking the Lower Bristol Road with Sainsbury's car park. Victoria Suspension Bridge, completed in 1836, is unusual in that its suspension rods are slanted – the designer, J. Dredge, submitted a similar concept for the Clifton Suspension Bridge competition. Churchill Bridge replaced Old Bridge in 1966; the abutments of the latter now carry the footbridge upstream of Churchill. The Churchill/Old Bridge area was once Bath's main quayside; it is still known locally as Broad Quay but, apart from a few outcrops of waterline stonework, there is no evidence of the cranes, wharves and warehouses that once saw the hustle and bustle of barges and narrowboats plying their trade.

Not surprisingly boaters and walkers have their own preferences when it comes to being more at home on or by still or moving waters. Whatever your inclination, Bath and the junction of canal and river heralds a change of mood and style: wide becomes narrow, deep becomes shallow; alternatively man-made becomes natural, cuttings and embankments become timeless meanderings. In between flurries of mellowing stone the river espies the worst of Bath; Roman remains and Georgian façades notwithstanding, the city had to earn a living and the remnants of decaying wharves and warehouses confirm the river as a major artery in the pursuit and creation of local wealth. Thus the old frontages are part of the city's industrial heritage … time will pass its own judgement on the hotch-potch of 20th-century infilling!

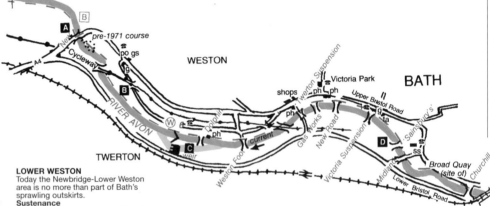

LOWER WESTON
Today the Newbridge-Lower Weston area is no more than part of Bath's sprawling outskirts.
Sustenance
DOLPHIN INN – home-cooked food in a local atmosphere; riverside by Dolphin Bridge.
THE BOATHOUSE – reasonably-priced restaurant offering comprehensive menu, including vegetarian and children's dishes, at splendid riverside location close to New Bridge. Casual moorings.

RIVERSIDE BATH
Bath itself features in greater detail on page 19; the information below relates to the river's north bank (the Upper Bristol Road) as this provides the only access to and from the water.
Sustenance
WINDSOR CASTLE – bar food; at the junction of Windsor Bridge and the main road.
NEW WESTHALL – bar snacks; opposite Victoria Park.
HOPE POLE INN – good selection of food; opposite Victoria Park.
PARK TAVERN – excellent cuisine; opposite entrance to Victoria Park.
Shops
Various, including a launderette and Sainsbury's supermarket, the latter right on the river.
Sightseeing
GREEN PARK STATION – now part of the Sainsbury complex, this, the former terminus of the Midland Railway in Bath, has been tastefully reclaimed and includes a small photographic display of times past. Now also the site of a medieval-style craft market.

For the Walker
Walking between Newbridge and Bath is straightforward, the Avon Walkway being well-signposted, particularly where it changes sides. The designated Cycleway (the old Midland Railway track bed) offers an alternative on its four 'points of contact' with the Walkway between Bitton and its terminus at Brassmill Lane near Weston Lock (6).

FOR THE BOATER
When approaching Sainsbury's Bridge from downstream be aware that oncoming craft may pass under via the 'wrong' arch.

All craft navigating the Avon should carry an anchor.

Always moor facing upstream when stopping for a prolonged period.

Avoid cruising or mooring on the river at times of excessive fresh water or flood.

Never leave a WINDLASS on a PADDLE SPINDLE.

Bath Marina, Brassmill Lane, Bath BA1 3JT; tel: Bath (01225) 424301. Water, pump-out, rubbish disposal, gas, diesel, boat & engine repairs, boat sales & brokerage, chandlery, food shop, insurance, moorings, lift-out, hard standing, laundry and shower facilities, K&A windlasses and BW keys.

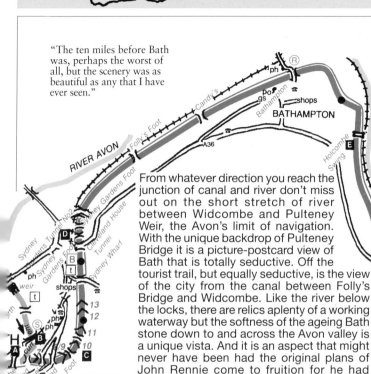

"The ten miles before Bath was, perhaps the worst of all, but the scenery was as beautiful as any that I have ever seen."

From whatever direction you reach the junction of canal and river don't miss out on the short stretch of river between Widcombe and Pulteney Weir, the Avon's limit of navigation. With the unique backdrop of Pulteney Bridge it is a picture-postcard view of Bath that is totally seductive. Off the tourist trail, but equally seductive, is the view of the city from the canal between Folly's Bridge and Widcombe. Like the river below the locks, there are relics aplenty of a working waterway but the softness of the ageing Bath stone down to and across the Avon valley is a unique vista. And it is an aspect that might never have been had the original plans of John Rennie come to fruition for he had surveyed a route that linked canal and river via a 5-lock flight between Bathampton and Batheaston Weir.

Restoration
Traffic was first stopped from entering Widcombe Locks (7-13) from the river in 1953. K&ACT volunteers worked on the locks in the 60s and 70s and Bath City Council gave £7,500 towards restoration. The flight was re-opened in 1976 (8 and 9 were amalgamated) but, due to lack of water, closed again until electric pumping operated at Claverton in 1982.

A Widcombe Bridge: The river footbridge downstream of the locks is known locally as 'Halfpenny' Bridge. It replaces a wooden cantilever toll bridge that collapsed in 1877, killing 11 of those waiting to pay their ¹/₂d toll.

B Allen's Wharf: Allen's Wharf, Dolemead, was the river terminus of a 1¹/₂ -mile horse-drawn railway down from Ralph Allen's Combe Down stone quarry. It flourished for 30 years during the rebuilding of Bath in the mid-18th century, handling, at its peak, two barges, each making four trips daily.

C Widcombe Locks: Two chimney stacks alongside the Widcombe Locks epitomize one of the major problems of the K&A – water supply. With lock-full after lock-full tumbling down into the Avon, and Claverton Pump (see below) unable to keep pace, two pumping stations, one – Thimble Mill (now a restaurant) – by Bottom Lock and the other alongside Abbey View Lock (11), reclaimed some of the canal's life-blood. The locks themselves are a treasure trove of canal memorabilia – iron bridges, rope-worn iron and stone work, a lock-keeper's cottage, stable buildings and maltsters. But most dramatic of all is the amalgamation of locks 8 and 9 as the awesome chamber of Bath Deep Lock (8/9), Britain's deepest canal lock.

D Sydney Gardens: Between Sydney and Darlington Wharves is an outpost of fashionable Bath, the almost secret walled-world of Sydney Gardens, its canal spanned by two ornate cast-iron bridges, 'Erected Anno 1800', and protected by two short tunnel-bridges. Above the southern tunnel stands Cleveland House, the original headquarters of the Canal Company.

E Hampton Quarry Wharf: Bath's Hampton Quarry (on the downs above) furnished much of the stone used on the canal. It was brought down by tramroad – much of which is still traceable – and when the canal opened here in 1808, was moved by barge to work still in place.

F Claverton Pumping Station: Today Claverton Pump is the key to the canal's water supply in the west with water drawn up from the indefatigable Avon being back-pumped up the lock flights. Built originally to augment the canal's water supply between Bradford and Bath, it was unique in that its two large water-wheels were themselves powered by the river.

FOR THE BOATER
The most picturesque (and therefore most public) moorings on the river at Bath are at Pulteney Weir; equally convenient are those just downstream of Churchill Bridge.

The Widcombe Locks are open daily 8.00am-4.30pm. All boats need to clear the flight by 6.00pm. Should you require help the lock-keeper is usually based at lock 11. Some of the locks have walkways on the inside of the gates; crews of longer craft locking up should ensure that they do not get caught under these as the lock fills.

Bath Narrowboats, Sydney Wharf, Bath BA2 4EL; tel: (01225) 447276. Water, gas, diesel, 'Elsan' disposal, pump-out, chandlery, boat sales, K&A windlasses, BW keys.

John Knill & Son, Hampton Wharf, Bathampton, Bath; tel: Bath (01225) 463603. Moorings.

WIDCOMBE
Although riverside Widcombe has been all but devastated by new roads, the main street retains much of its charm.
Sustenance
RAM – renovated boatman's hostelry with good food.
RING O'BELLS – small local with bar snacks in friendly atmosphere.
ROYAL OAK – known locally as 'Rossiter's' after a long-serving landlord; open all day; bar food.
STAKIS BATH HOTEL – new canalside complex incorporating the renovated Thimble Mill as an up-market restaurant.
Sightseeing
Halfpenny Bridge – over 100 years of flood levels are etched on the bridge's southern pier.

BATHAMPTON
A small canalside village that used to boast the Harbutt's Plasticine works; it was to the local inn that the dying loser of Britain's last *legal* dual, Viscount du Barry, was brought.

Sustenance
GEORGE INN – local popular for its food and canalside setting.
Sightseeing
ST NICHOLAS' CHURCH – Admiral Phillip, first Governor of New South Wales, lies buried in the so-called 'Australian Chapel'.

CLAVERTON
A quiet village nestling, almost unnoticed, behind the A36.
Sightseeing
AMERICAN MUSEUM, CLAVERTON MANOR – home to a Museum of American decorative arts and life between the 17th and 19th centuries; open Easter-Oct (ex Mon), tel: Bath (01225) 460503.
CLAVERTON PUMP – open every Sunday and Bank Holiday from Easter to end October with special 'running' weekends; details from Bath (01225) 483001.
Public Transport
ROAD – regular Badgerline services to/from Claverton and Bathampton; details from Bath (01225) 464446.

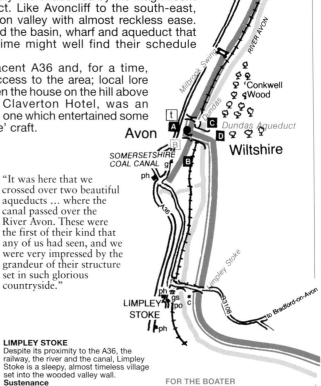

A Dundas Wharf: Its proximity to the A36 ensures that Dundas Wharf and its environs are today a focal point for visitors to the canal. Sufficient artefacts remain – a stone warehouse, a wharfside crane, a tiny toll office, a grooved iron corner post – to feed the imagination. The junction with the Somersetshire Coal Canal completes the picture, the narrow entrance lock now restored as access to private moorings. It is clear that this lock was once broad and led to a wider wharf beyond and that Dundas Wharf dates from the 1820s, presumably in response to the 'narrowing' of the SCC lock. What whims or rivalries led to these changes can be no more than speculation.

B Somersetshire Coal Canal: Like the Kennet & Avon, the SCC was a product of the canal mania of the late 18th century. Although separate companies, work on the two was being carried out simultaneously, with the Somerset collieries eager to gain access to the wider market that the K&A offered. The SCC is perhaps best known for its infamous and short-lived caisson lock, a Heath Robinson-like contrivance which, it was hoped, would obviate the need for locks. But locks it had to be – 22 of them at Combe Hay, completed in 1805. One hundred years later, all traffic had ceased with much of the bed becoming Camerton & Limpley Stoke Railway, the location in the 50s for the film *The Titfield Thunderbolt*.

C Dundas Aqueduct: As a canal engineer, John Rennie's skills have often been held suspect but no-one can deny the magnificence, even audacity, of his aqueducts. Dundas (on the Avon/Wiltshire county boundary) is one of two on the K&A that captures the imagination. Though shorter than Avoncliff, the setting is more dramatic, the canal's doric columns – despite the ravages of time on the downstream face – totally at one with their environment.

D Conkwell Wharf and Quarry: The Wiltshire end of Dundas Aqueduct once boasted a small wharf served by a tramroad from Conkwell Quarry above. The stone was of inferior quality and caused problems when used in the canal's construction; quarrying was thus soon discontinued.

The purlieus of the Limpley Stoke valley are a place for superlatives and yet even the overseeing green or rustic richness of Conkwell Wood to the east is itself partially overshadowed by the magnificent boldness of Dundas Aqueduct. Like Avoncliff to the south-east, Dundas strides across the Avon valley with almost reckless ease. There is so much to see around the basin, wharf and aqueduct that anyone with an eye to the time might well find their schedule temporarily thwarted.

The canal predates the adjacent A36 and, for a time, provided the least arduous access to the area; local lore has it that there was a time when the house on the hill above Dundas Wharf Bridge, the Claverton Hotel, was an establishment of 'ill repute' and one which entertained some of the canal's earliest 'pleasure' craft.

Restoration
In 1960 boats attending a rally at Bathampton cruised to Dundas; thereafter, until 1982, Hampton Quarry Wharf was the limit of navigation – see page 21. The early 80s found Dundas Aqueduct leaking until, following Heath Robinson-ish repairs, it was relined and re-opened in 1984 to link Bristol and Bradford. The 'dry section' was drained in 1954 and remained thus until relined under a K&ACT/BW/MSC/Wilts County Council scheme in the 70s.

"It was here that we crossed over two beautiful aqueducts ... where the canal passed over the River Avon. These were the first of their kind that any of us had seen, and we were very impressed by the grandeur of their structure set in such glorious countryside."

'DUNDAS'
Dundas does not exist as a geographical location; nevertheless within the sub-culture of the waterways the cluster of houses within the canals to the east have a certain Dundas-ness.
Sustenance
ANGELFISH – home-made food and cakes; 10.00am-6.00pm every day and Friday and Saturday evenings; beside the SCC Interpretation Centre (see below).
VIADUCT HOTEL – good value bar food and B&B; on the A36 ¼ mile south of Dundas Wharf.
Shops
TITFIELD THUNDERBOLT – small but extensively stocked bookshop covering transport and local guides; also many canal-related gifts; beside the SCC Interpretation Centre (see below).
Sightseeing
SOMERSETSHIRE COAL CANAL INTERPRETATION CENTRE – displays and information focusing on the history of the Somersetshire Coal Canal at the end of a short, restored section of that canal which joins the K&A at Dundas.

LIMPLEY STOKE
Despite its proximity to the A36, the railway, the river and the canal, Limpley Stoke is a sleepy, almost timeless village set into the wooded valley wall.
Sustenance
HOP POLE INN – known locally for its food; ¼ mile south-west of Limpley Stoke Bridge.
NIGHTINGALES – popular local Italian restaurant; open Tuesday to Saturday evenings and for Sunday lunch – tel: Bath (01225) 723150; by the river bridge.
FORDSIDE TEA GARDEN – cream teas and cakes; just south of Limpley Stoke Bridge.
Sightseeing
ST MARY'S CHURCH – a special feature is the Church's display of 13th-15th-century tomb covers ... dead interesting, too!
FRESHFORD – this picturesque, even quaint and rather up-market village clings to the slopes of the narrow valley south of Limpley Stoke at the confluence of the rivers Avon and Frome – the medieval stone bridge over the latter is particularly attractive.
Public Transport
ROAD – local Badgerline service to/from Dundas and Limpley Stoke; details from Bath (01225) 464446.

FOR THE BOATER
Some swing bridges can only be unlocked with a windlass.

A BREAKING WASH damages the banks

Always SLOW DOWN when passing MOORED CRAFT

Bath & Dundas Canal Company, Brass Knocker Basin, Monkton Combe, Bath BA2 7JD; tel: Bath (01225) 722292. Day boats, gas, diesel (24-hours notice), pump-out (24-hours notice), 'Elsan' disposal, slipway, boat sales & brokerage, moorings, K&A windlasses, BW keys, car parking and B&B.

Chris's Boat Services, Brass Knocker Basin, Monkton Combe, Bath BA2 7JD; tel: Bath (01225) 722226. Boat & engine repairs, servicing, dry dock, chandlery.

'Picturesque' and 'scenic' seem somehow inadequate appendages to a description of the Limpley Stoke valley. 'Sylvan' and 'resplendent' are closer to the mark; even with the intrusion of the occasional train this is a peaceful place, its almost magical quality quite seductive. True, there is the tiny canalside settlement at Avoncliff and its *raison d'être*, the imposing, nay audacious, Avoncliff Aqueduct leaping across the valley with the same grace and strength as its western neighbour, Dundas. Walkers get the best view for the towpath changes sides here by going under the aqueduct's southern arch, though it is by no means a wasted journey to first take in the view up-valley from its east-facing walkway. Bradford-on-Avon can and must not be missed and features on page 28.

Restoration

Dewatered in 1954, the 'dry section' was relined with polythene and concrete by 1978. The first passage of boats between Dundas and Bradford was in 1984 – following the relining of Dundas and Avoncliff Aqueducts in the early 80s. Bradford Lock (14) was first padlocked in 1951; it was restored in 1978 and opened in 1985. By 1986 back-pumping was operable to maintain water levels above.

A The 'Dry Section': the so-called 'dry section' between Limpley Stoke Bridge and Avoncliff should, modern materials permitting, never again be 'dry'. Clinging to the valley wall, the Bath-Bradford section was prone to leakage and landslips but it was east of Limpley Stoke (witness the surfeit of stop-gates and planks) that stoppages became almost annual with maintenance gangs 'puddling' their way over the cracks. Walkers might keep a weather eye open for one sceptic's etching on the concrete edge … "I'LL BET IT LEAKS".

B Murhill Quarry Wharf: In the 18th and 19th centuries Bath stone was a much sought-after commodity; it was thus not surprising that the K&A begat several transhipment wharves. Here at Murhill, evidence of past activity is well preserved – not so the stone from the quarry above which, as evidenced by the northern face of Dundas Aqueduct, was of poor quality.

C Avoncliff Aqueduct: Somehow the modern relining of Avoncliff Aqueduct seems at variance with the spectacular leap of its stone balustrading across the Avon valley. The eastern façade has a definite sag and boasts numerous brick repairs but neither detracts from this monument to Rennie's genius. Upstream are two flock mills, one restored as a private residence, the other, its access axed by the railway, a decaying relic of another age.

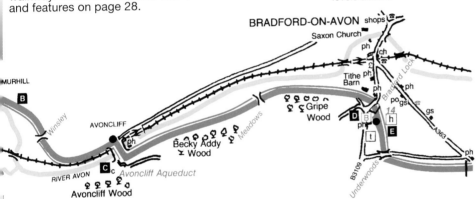

BRADFORD-ON-AVON

36-acre park and Tithe Barn feature in the circular walk described on page 60.

BRADFORD-ON-AVON

Details of this erstwhile wool-town feature on page 28; canalside facilities only are outlined below.
Sustenance
CANAL TAVERN – refurbished traditional canalside pub; pub grub; by Lower Wharf.
BARGE INN – food and B&B available in this large hostelry with canalside beer garden; by Frome Wharf.
BEEHIVE – bar food and B&B in friendly local atmosphere; canalside at Widbrook Bridge.
LOCK INN COTTAGE – all-day menu ('boatman's breakfast') and evening meals at weekend in cheerful, welcoming café; canalside terrace by Lower Wharf; also day-boat, canoe and cycle hire.
Public Transport
RAIL – services to/from Bradford-on-Avon and (very infrequently) Avoncliff Halt (on the Bath-Westbury line); details on 0345 484950 .
ROAD – local Badgerline service to/from Bradford-on-Avon; details from Bath (01225) 464446.

D Bradford Lock and Wharves: It was at Bradford-on-Avon that the first sod was cut in the name of the Kennet & Avon in October 1794. In its heyday, the site boasted two wharves, one (Frome Road) above and one (Lower) below the lock. Relics of both abound and their respective hostelry – from the crane pedestal and loading bays of the lower to the gauging dock (now a dry dock) and wharfinger's house of the upper. Before the innovation of Bath Deep Lock (8/9), Bradford Lock (14), with a rise/fall of 12ft 6in, was the canal's deepest.

E Bradford Clay Farm: Puddling clay (the canal's bed) doesn't grow on trees … and it's an even rarer commodity hereabouts now that Bradford's canalside 'farm' has been dug dry.

I'LL BET IT LEAKS PRD 1978

FOR THE BOATER
Some swing bridges can only be unlocked with a windlass.

If you are making a WASH you are going TOO FAST

Kennet & Avon Canal Trust, Frome Road Wharf, Bradford-on-Avon; tel (01380) 868683. Water, gas, diesel, 'Elsan' disposal, rubbish disposal, pump-out, dry dock, moorings, BW keys, café.

AVONCLIFF
This tiny hamlet has its roots in the local weaving industry, though, in its turn, the canal brought its attendant community.
Sustenance
CROSS GUNS – a popular olde worlde hostelry with excellent food and B&B; be-tween canal and river east of the aqueduct. TEAZELS – licensed café, cream teas; attractive garden seating immediately west of Avoncliff aqueduct.
Sightseeing
BARTON FARM COUNTRY PARK – the

A Dorset & Somerset Canal: The canal age begat successes and failures. The Kennet & Avon, the Somersetshire Coal Canal (see page 22) and the Wilts & Berks (see opposite) were, initially at least, the former; by contrast all work had ceased on the Dorset & Somerset by 1803 through lack of funds. Had it been completed, the line from near Sturminster Newton via Wincanton and Frome would have joined the K&A at Widbrook.

B River Avon: The Avon's circuitous route to the canal at Bath begins far off on the Gloucester-Wiltshire border (there are at least three recognisable sources) and takes in Malmesbury, Chippenham, Lacock and Melksham; its course through the last three was advocated as a possible route for the proposed Western Canal. John Rennie's survey of 1973 changed all that and instead the higher, more southerly route that saw fruition as the K&A, here affords open views across the gentle slopes of the meandering Avon valley.

C Biss Aqueduct: The classical span of the aqueduct over the river Biss, a tributary of the Avon, is scarcely in the same league as Rennie's more spectacular creations to the west at Avoncliff and Dundas – see pages 22 and 23. Nevertheless, on any other canal it would be considered individual, even stylish, and is worth the scramble down the bank for a closer look. Its neighbour carries the railway under the canal and is, of course, a later addition, though its robust stone façade is entirely in keeping with the K&A's 'style'.

D Hilperton Wharves: It is not easy to visualise what remains of the two Hilperton wharves as a busy canalside scene. Situated on either side of the B3105 road bridge, they served Trowbridge which, though originally on the canal's proposed route, was passed by in the interests of economy. The subsequent suggested branch to the town was also shelved. Marsh Wharf, east of the bridge, was active as early as 1805 with the Trowbridge area being one of the first to benefit from the cheaper fuel brought from the Somerset coalfields.

The views north across the valley of the meandering Avon are either your first glimpses of the river or a fond farewell to it – it all depends on whether you are travelling east-west or west-east. For a time the canal clings even more precariously to the valley wall, tall poplars screening the view south. Here too there is wildlife in abundance: mallard, muscovy duck, swans and moorhens – the latter, so one suspect local 'source' has it, so-named because they are "more hen than duck"! Bradford's Bath stone and Trowbridge's industrial outskirts vie for your attention and while the one looms and the other recedes think on the irony that, before the re-opening of the canal hereabouts, many of Trowbridge's townsfolk were unsure how the *Canal Road* Industrial Estate got its name!

> "The weeds (around Hilperton) had been particularly bad, and we had been towing the boat for several miles in bitterly cold weather and were all feeling tired and irritable, when it suddenly started to rain in torrents."

Restoration
Being lock-less, the Bradford-on-Avon-Semington section never fell into the advanced state of disrepair that afflicted other parts of the canal. Weeding and silting were more of a problem and this was in part alleviated around Hilperton by WIN-sponsored dredging – see opposite. By the late 70s, two trip-boats plying the stretch from opposite ends, kept things on the move.

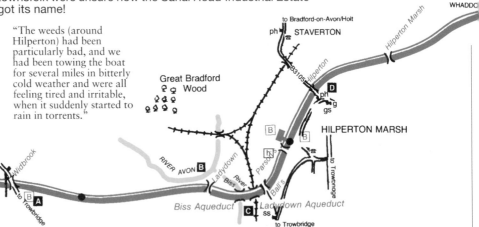

Public Transport
ROAD – local Badgerline to/from Hilperton; details from Bath (01225) 464446.

HILPERTON MARSH
Part of Hilperton itself, a scattered village that just, but only just, retains its separate identity now that Trowbridge (Wiltshire's administrative centre) has expanded. Only its north-western fringes touch the canal.
Sustenance
KING'S ARMS – a large modernised inn-cum-eating-place; canalside by Hilperton Bridge.
Shops
There is a discount food store ¾ mile south of Balls Bridge, in Canal Road.

STAVERTON
An erstwhile, albeit small, weaving centre on the river Avon, dominated today by the tall red stack of the Nestlé factory. In another life (as a clothing factory) it boasted the first power-loom in the district; three-storey terraces of weavers' cottages, similar to those in Yorkshire, remain.
Sustenance
OLD BEAR INN – good food in a typical village pub; on the B3105, ¼ mile north-west of Hilperton Bridge.

FOR THE BOATER
Bradford-on-Avon Marina, Trowbridge Road, Bradford-on-Avon BA15 1UD; tel: (01225) 864562. Water, 'Elsan' disposal, pump-out, gas, diesel, slipway, boat and engine sales & repair, boat brokerage, moorings, BW licences, restaurant.

Sally Boats, Bradford-on-Avon Marina, Trowbridge Road, Bradford-on-Avon BA15 1UD; tel: (01225) 864923. 2-10 berth hire boats, dry dock, basic chandlery, K&A windlasses, BW keys.

Wessex Narrowboats, Wessex Wharf, Hilperton, Trowbridge BA14 8RS; tel: Trowbridge (01225) 769847. 2-8 berth hire-craft, water, boat & engine repairs and servicing, fitting out, cranage, dry and wet dock, narrowboat day-hire.

Hilperton Marina, Hammond Way, Trowbridge BA14 8RS; tel: Trowbridge (01225) 765243. Water, 'Elsan' disposal, pump-out, rubbish disposal, gas, diesel, slipway, boat and engine repairs, servicing & sales, insurance, moorings, chandlery, K&A windlasses, BW keys.

Semington's two locks and the adjacent road bridge are almost the sole intruders in this largely agricultural terrain. Occasionally the open farmland exudes a windswept wildness, a natural habitat for hedgerow fruits such as elderberry and blackberry, rosehip and hawthorn ... everything, it seems except the elusive sloe. All in all a veritable haven for jam, syrup and wine makers. One other canal artefact goes almost unnoticed – the impressively robust, albeit squat, stone aqueduct that crosses Semington Brook. Like many aqueducts, no matter how spectacular, it is easy – particularly for boaters – to miss out on the view ... not *from* it, but *of* it. To scramble down the bank inevitably involves tying-up and a possible break in schedule – but on this canal it is never a wasted exercise!

Restoration
Buckley's and Barrett's Locks (15 and 16) at Semington fell into disrepair during the 50s and 60s and were restored during the late 70s – though were not brought into use until the summer of 1985 when Maintenance Agreements with the local authorities were established. A back-pump was installed in 1987 to maintain water levels between Semington and Seend flights.

A Semington Aqueduct:
The aqueduct spanning Semington Brook is the smallest of four that cross the Avon or its tributaries; it is, nonetheless, impressively robust, though somewhat squat.

B Semington Wharf:
It was at Semington Wharf that traffic to and from the Wilts & Berks Canal 'clocked in', the main 'export' trade being in Somerset Coal.

C Wilts & Berks Canal:
What was once the busy junction of two canals is today strangely, almost eerily, impotent; it is not unknown for boaters and walkers alike to pass by oblivious to any such union. The junction's towpath bridge is scarcely recognisable as such, while the stop lock and the line of the canal lie under the garden of the old toll house. This narrow canal was no minor undertaking; its 51 miles – completed by 1810 – via Melksham, Lacock and Swindon, joined the Thames at Abingdon, while the North Wilts Canal linked Swindon with the Thames & Severn by 1819. Railway competition and the many locks eventually strangled trade, the 10,000 tons of Somerset coal that passed through to Abingdon in 1837 a short-lived hiatus. By 1906 all traffic had ceased.

D Wiltshire Inland Navigators:
In the 1970s Semington Lock and the then occupant of the lock cottage, Len Brown, brought controversy to the restoration of the K&A. Len was not inclined to let the grass grow under his feet and was, like others before and since, not always in agreement with the K&A Trust and its, as he saw it, lethargic approach to the canal's restoration. With others, Len formed Wiltshire Inland Navigators and it must be said that, despite opposition from within both the Trust and BW, WIN succeeded in hastening restoration of the length towards Trowbridge.

E Littleton Mill:
It is ironic that one of Wiltshire's worst machine-breaking riots should have taken place at Littleton Mill in 1802, a stone's throw away from the virgin cut of the K&A. The canal brought more changes to the area than the rioters could have envisaged and the mill was to have strong connections with it, including, as recently as the 1930s, its own wharf with narrowboats carrying grain between Avonmouth and the linking tramroad.

FOR THE BOATER
Some swing bridges can only be unlocked with a windlass.

Never leave a WINDLASS on a PADDLE SPINDLE

Remember to SLOW DOWN when passing FISHERMEN

Wilts Marine Services, Witchcroft, Kingsdown, Corsham SN13 8BT; tel: Bath (01225) 742241. Water, rubbish disposal, cranage, dry and wet dock, boat and engine repairs, servicing and sales, insurance surveys, chandlery, K&A windlasses, BW keys.

Wilderness Boats, Stokes Road, Corsham SN13 9AA; tel: Corsham (01249) 712231. Trailable boat building, boat and engine spares & sales, chandlery.

tranquil boats, Lock House, Semington, Melksham BA14 6JT; tel: Devizes (01380) 870 654. Electric day-boat hire, slipway, covered DIY dry dock, trailboat storage.

SEMINGTON
A small, compact village north-west of the Melksham-Westbury and Devizes-Trowbridge crossroads. Despite the proximity of the motor car, it is an attractive hamlet with many fine 18th-century houses.

St George's Hospital started life as the local workhouse.

Sustenance
SOMERSET ARMS – excellent home-made food; ¼ mile south of Semington Bridge.

Sightseeing
WILTS & BERKS CANAL – a short walk north from Semington Bridge along the A350 reveals, to the east just beyond the farm buildings (the original toll house), about 100 yds of the Wilts & Berks; at certain times of the year it proves it can still hold water.
LITTLETON MILL – a public footpath leaving the A350 almost opposite the *Somerset Arms* leads to Littleton Mill (1 mile). In 1802 there was a fulling and spinning mill here, one of two in the area that became victim to the machine-breaking riots. The mill was burnt down and one Thomas Elleker tried and executed for arson.

Public Transport
ROAD – local Badgerline services Chippenham, Devizes and Trowbridge; details from Bath (01225) 464446.

A Seend Wharf: The *Barge Inn* and the neighbouring stone house are virtually all that remains of Seend Wharf. The inn, only recently modernised, had strong canal connections, not only as a mid-flight watering hole for passing boatmen but also as stabling for their tireless horses.

B Seend Iron Works: Even more elusive than Seend Wharf is the site of the short-lived iron workings that for a mere 30 years, in the latter part of the 19th century, provided employment locally and financial insecurity for a succession of owners. Ore was smelted in two blast furnaces on a site linked by tramroad with the canal and eventually across the canal to the railway. The lines of both tramways remain clearly definable, their peaceful, verdant setting belying their industrial origins. The terrace of erstwhile iron-worker's cottages north of Seend Wharf Bridge are in sharp contrast to the splendidly-named iron-master's house, *Ferrum Towers*, on the hillside to the south.

C Scott's and Wragg's Wharves: Little tangible evidence remains of either Scott's or Wragg's Wharves; a close look at the OS map confirms that a right-of-way remains from the site of the former up to Seend village. Activity ceased at Wragg's Wharf when, in 1898, trade from the Somerset collieries ended; two narrowboats had regularly plied between Dunkerton Colliery and the wharf.

D Martinslade Wharf: It is easier to visualise wharf-side trade here than at either Scott's or Wragg's to the west. Nevertheless, though the Bath stone house and warehousing remain, the short arm that 'fed' the wharf is long gone.

The hilltop settlement of Seend Cleeve and the attendant lock flight are set amid the tranquillity of rolling hills and scattered farm buildings. The abundance of swing-bridges is evidence that the canal came as an intrusion, a raw scar cut through old farming communities and their rural pre-occupations. But the scars have healed and even the more industrial backdrop that was borne out of the canal hereabouts is today but a memory treasured by the few. Be prepared to pass – or be passed by – reedy islands drifting along the cut, some large enough to harbour the inscrutable Japanese warrior, lone and ageing, awaiting the end of hostilities. Fear not … for there are more than a few wartime pill-boxes to which to beat a hasty – if disbelieving – retreat.

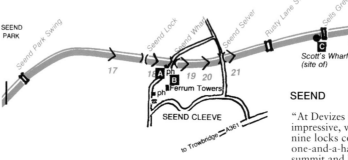

SEEND

SEEND CLEEVE
It is Seend Cleeve rather than Seend that touches the canal. It is a largely agricultural community, clinging to the hillside that once thrived from its ironstone workings.
Sustenance
BARGE INN – until recently a step back in time, though the refurbishment is not out of character; good home-cooked food; canalside by Seend Wharf Bridge.
BREWERY INN – good food (except Sunday) and draught cider; ¼ mile south of Seend Wharf Bridge.

SEEND
In 1684 the antiquary John Aubrey wrote of Seend: "I know not any small country village that has so many well-built houses." Some of those he espied remain today along the main street, memorials to the wealth created locally from the cloth industry; no less attractive are the humbler weavers' cottages.
Sustenance
BELL INN – home-made food and bar snacks; ³/₄ mile south of Seend Selver Bridge on the A361.

Restoration
Like most of the navigation's locks, the Seend flight (17-21) suffered from increasing deprivation during and from the 50s. Restoration work began in 1978 and was soon completed but, like Semington, the locks remained unused until 1985 when navigation through Bradford Lock (14) was agreed. A back-pump was installed in 1987 to maintain water levels between Seend and Lower Foxhangers.

"At Devizes the sudden descent is most impressive, with a staircase of twenty-nine locks confined to the space of one-and-a-half miles. Standing at the summit and looking down the locks, the structure of the gate arms resembled the backbone of a huge fish."

SELLS GREEN
A cluster of well-kept houses hiding behind the main A365.
Sustenance
THREE MAGPIES – excellent food in olde worlde surroundings; ¼ mile north from Sells Green Bridge.
Public Transport
ROAD – local Badgerline services; details from Bath (01225) 464446.

FOR THE BOATER
Boaters are advised not to moor overnight in a flight of locks.

Some swing bridges can only be unlocked with a windlass.

Equinox Boatbuilders, The Old Sawmill, Sells Green, Melksham SN12 6RS; tel: Devizes (01380) 828200. Steel narrowboat building, repairs and refits.

Clearly the locks climbing up to or down from Devizes – and in particular the Caen Hill flight – dominate the scene. Whatever the direction or mode of travel, the observer cannot but be awestruck by the audacity of such man-made monuments to the canal age. That said, the setting is pastoral and the natural elevation affords splendid uninterrupted views towards Melksham and Chippenham and the Avon valley. West of Lower Foxhangers the cut crosses, almost unnoticed, the small Summerham Brook; insignificant it might seem but the Brook is tapped about ½ mile upstream to join the canal just east of Martinslade Wharf as the Seend Feeder. A canal in water may seem to be the natural order of things but now, as in the canal's heyday, 'feeding' the cut means extracting very drop of available water from the local environment.

Restoration
Closed in 1951, the increasing decay to the Devizes flight was stemmed in the early 70s by the K&ACT's removal of vegetation from the masonry. Restoration work, sponsored by BW and Kennet District Council, began in 1978. Steel top gates (except for 50) were fitted in 1981 with 'cranked' balance beams which were replaced before the re-opening of the flight by HM Queen Elizabeth II in August 1990.

A Wilts, Somerset & Weymouth Railway: The forlorn piers that flank and divide the canal at Lower Foxhangers are the frustrating remains of a bridge carrying the defunct Devizes branch of the Wilts, Somerset & Weymouth Railway. What a pity the bed could not have been saved for amenity use as with the Midland Railway west of Bath (see page 20).

B Devizes Lock Flight: Devizes' 29 locks can be divided into three distinct groups: seven at Foxhangers, 16 closely-grouped on Caen Hill and 6 between the latter and the town … a rise/fall of 234ft in 2¼ miles. All six road bridges that cross the east and west groupings have a separate towpath arch which probably facilitated the tramroad that linked top and bottom while work continued on the locks – a feature that, though aesthetically pleasing, must have caused problems to horse-drawn craft. Boats could work through the flight at night (the K&A's own gasworks was sited west of the cottages at lock 26) on payment of an extra shilling.

C Marsh Hill Wharf: The house by lock 28 was once occupied by John Blackwell, one of the Canal Company's first engineers; his contribution is commemorated on a plaque on the west face of Prison Bridge as well as in the more spectacular edifice of Crofton Pumping Station – see page 36. The triangular basin above the lock was edged by wharves as well as being a side pond (see below), which on the towpath side served the Canal Company's brickworks behind the lower Caen Hill locks – some relics remain.

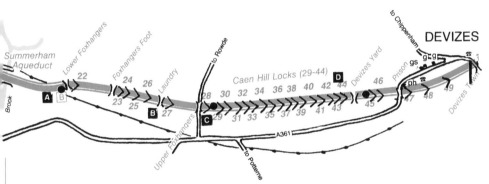

D Caen Hill: It was the completion of the Devizes locks in 1810 that finally saw the realisation of a project begun at Bradford-on-Avon and Newbury in 1794. The Caen Hill locks were the crowning glory, 16 audacious steps up the steep hillside that have been likened to a giant's vertebrae. With their water-storage side-ponds and magnificent symmetry, the Caen Hill locks more than justify L.T.C. Rolt's labelling as "the most spectacular lock flight in England". Boatmen soon discovered, however, the peculiarity of lock 41 … it is the narrowest on the canal.

DEVIZES
Detailed information on Devizes is on page 29; the following relates to canalside facilities only.
Sustenance
BLACK HORSE – bar snacks in the only 'in-flight' pub; canalside by Manifold Lock (47).

LOCK COTTAGE – Open 12.00-6.00, April-October for cream teas, snacks & ices; right beside Lock 44.
Public Transport
ROAD – local Badgerline services along A361; details from Bath (01225) 464446.

BRADFORD-ON-AVON

Bradford-on-Avon has been described as a clone of Bath … albeit to a much smaller mould. True, both exude the softness of the local freestone and both share the same canal, the same river and the same penchant for showing off their antiquity. But Bradford-on-Avon can stand on its own feet, it does not need to bask in the shadow of its larger, grander neighbour … it *is* a sight worth seeing.

The town perches precariously on the Avon's valley wall, its mellow-yellow terraces overseeing the river's 'broad ford' and its medieval replacement, a strong stone bridge complete with pilgrim's chapel, the town's lock-up in more recent times.

The wool industry was the basis of local wealth with the area once boasting as many as 32 mills. Ironically, it was the industry's leanings towards quality that led to its decline for, among others, its Yorkshire namesake was able to produce a cheaper product and consequently attract a wider market. Some riverside mills remain as custodians of more modern industries, while the stylish houses of erstwhile clothiers contrast with

the more functional – though nonetheless sought-after – weavers' cottages.

Two giant steps back further into the mists of time reveal the stone vastness of the 14th-century Tithe Barn and the early 8th-century simplicity of the Saxon Church of St Lawrence … both unique, both unforgettable and both featured in the circular walk described on page 60.

Shopping
Most of the basics are here. There are Lloyd's and Midland Banks.

Sustenance
There is something to cater for most tastes, though within each the choice can be limited. The following details do not include the several hostelry and eating places north of the river.

Pubs
THREE HORSESHOES – excellent pub grub in spacious surroundings 'twixt canal and town.
RIVERSIDE INN – extensive menu and courtyard tables plus accommodation; just off the St Margaret's Street car park.

Eating Out
GEORGIAN LODGE – excellent and varied menu; behind a classical façade overlooking Town Bridge.
UPOHAR – tandoori restaurant and take-away; just south of Lower Wharf.
THAI BARN – extensive menu of Royal Thai cuisine; set meals and *à la carte*; in Bridge Street, by the river.
MILL HOUSE – large family restaurant and bar within the Bradford-on-Avon Marina at Widbrook.

Sightseeing
The following are in addition to the various sights detailed in the walk described on page 60.
ABBEY MILL – this tall riverside mill, the last to be built, can be seen by looking downstream from Town Bridge.
TORY – this, the highest terrace of houses on the slopes of Conigre Hill to the north of the river, offers a variety of unexpected and exhilarating panoramas and includes the 15th-century St Mary's Chapel.

Information
TOURIST INFORMATION CENTRE – 34 Silver Street, Bradford-on-Avon, BA15 1JX; tel: Bradford-on-Avon (01225) 865797.

Public Transport
RAIL – Bradford-on-Avon, St Margaret's Street; tel: 0345 484950.
ROAD – Badgerline services to/from Bath and Trowbridge; tel: Bath (01225) 464446.

DEVIZES

The 19th-century writer, William Black, described Devizes thus: "If there is any deader town than Devizes in this country or any other, the present writer has no acquaintance with it." It must be said that the work was one of fiction and that the writer-cum-traveller had just experienced the delights of Bath and Bradford-on-Avon, compared with which such a view could be seen in terms of culture shock. Devizes does not pretend to be a Bath or a Bradford; its forte was as a market town, the large market place and its attendant 18th-century buildings a focal point.

Shortly after the Norman Conquest a hill-top castle was built where the ancient manors of Rowde, Cannings and Potterne converged – *ad divisas* (at the boundaries) as one Latin chronicler put it. The castle site has seen three changes in style: the original wooden structure was destroyed by fire in the early 12th century, its more robust replacement met an equally ignominious end at the hands of Cromwell, its remains becoming in turn the foundations for the extant 19th-century folly-like castellated mansion.

Many of the town's handsome buildings date from the same period when the wool trade locally was in the ascendancy. A number, such as the *Bear Hotel*, are hostelries that seem to have a direct pipeline to the local Wadworth's Brewery. The *Bear* and its next-door neighbour, the Corn Exchange, oversee the broad market place where an inscription on the Cross relates the cautionary tale of one Ruth Pierce who met an untimely death here upon telling a lie ... a deader town than Devizes... ?

Shopping
Devizes has all the basics. Though the Market Place was clearly once the focus of commercial life, the centres of shopping are today more scattered and include some traffic-free areas. That said, everything is within a few minutes walk of the wharf.

Sustenance
There are many fine hostelries from which to choose – many, not surprisingly, offering the local Wadworth's brew. The choice of restaurants is more limited, though many of the pubs also do excellent food.

Pubs
ROYAL OAK – a good range of bar food in the nearest town pub to the wharf.
OLD CROWN – homely atmosphere; just south of the wharf.
CASTLE – large hostelry with B&B and a range of food to suit all tastes; in New Park Street, south-east of the wharf.
BEAR – excellent range of food in this imposing and historic inn-cum-hotel in the Market Place.

Eating Out
FOUR SEASONS – popular eatery with ever-changing, but always interesting menu; in High Street, just south-east of Market Place.
WHARFSIDE FOOD & CRAFTS – fairly large restaurant serving country-style food; alongside Devizes Wharf in Couch Lane.
D.D.'s – a homely 'tea-rooms' atmosphere with good down-to-earth fare; south-east of the wharf in New Park Street.
WILTSHIRE KITCHEN – recommended eatery specialising in good value home-made dishes in St John's Street.

Entertainment
WHARF THEATRE – Devizes Wharf; tel: Devizes (01380) 724741.
PALACE CINEMA – Northgate Street; tel: Devizes (01380) 722971.

Exhibitions/Museums
DEVIZES WHARF CANAL CENTRE – the headquarters of the Canal Trust doubles as an interpretative centre, bookshop and museum for the K&A and waterways in general; tel: Devizes (01380) 729849.
DEVIZES MUSEUM –the museum of the Wiltshire Archaeological and Natural History Society, including excellent exhibitions on local history; in Long Street; tel: Devizes (01380) 727369.

Sightseeing
MARKET PLACE – a plethora of imposing (mostly 18th-century) buildings, representatives of a variety of architectural styles. The Market Cross tells the story of Ruth Pierce's death in 1753.
ST JOHN'S CHURCH – a blend of Norman and more ornate 15th-century work; well worth a visit if only because the churchyard affords the best views of the (private) Victorian mansion that is Devizes Castle.
THE GREAT PORCH HOUSE – next to D.d.'s, and the overhanging timber-framed houses of the cobbled St John's Alley are worthy of more than a passing glance.

Information
TOURIST INFORMATION CENTRE – Cromwell House, Market Place, Devizes SN10 1JG; tel: Devizes (01380) 729408.

Public Transport
ROAD – Badgerline services to/from Salisbury, Westbury and Bath; tel: Bath (01225) 464446. Infrequent Wilts & Dorset services to villages to east; tel: Salisbury (01722) 336855.

A Devizes' Wharves: In its heyday Devizes boasted three wharves: one below Town Bridge, Sussex Wharf; one just above Kennet Lock (50), Lower Wharf; and Town Wharf which, being the only real survivor, is generally known today as Devizes Wharf. That said, it doesn't take much imagination to recreate the busy scene that was once the norm between the rear of the Wadworth's complex and Cemetery Road Bridge. Two restored buildings remain on the wharf. One, a warehouse that used to boast a crane, now houses the local Wharf Theatre while the long building at right angles to the canal began life as a granary, became a bonded ware-house for wine (where stored goods awaited payment of customs' duty), and now doubles as the Kennet & Avon Trust's headquarters, information centre, shop and museum.

B Kennet & Avon Trust: The inland Waterways Association was formed in 1946, committing itself to stem the tide of deterioration that, through lack of Government and public support, was enveloping Britain's inland waterways network. The IWA's Kennet & Avon branch was formed in 1948 and in 1951 became an independent body, The Kennet & Avon Canal Association, its aim being to prevent the canal falling further into disrepair. In response to a proposed Bill to close the navigation, a 20,000-signature petition was presented to the Queen in 1956; the Bill was to fail on its Second Reading, and a further two years elapsed before a Report on all inland waterways was published. The Bowes Report was in favour of the 'redevelopment' of, among others, the K&A, but its recommendations were not acted upon other than in the formation of the Inland Waterways Redevelopment Advisory Committee. In 1962 a further report, this time by IWRAC, proposed that the British Transport Waterways (reconstituted as BWB in 1963, now BW) and the K&ACA jointly undertake the canal's restoration as a result of which the K&ACA reformed itself as a registered charity, The Kennet & Avon Canal Trust.

C Devizes Sand Company: Lurking behind the towpath by Brickham Bridge were the Devizes Sand Company's pits. High-quality sand was shipped by canal to Stothert & Pitt's riverside engineering works in Bath where it was used in the iron-moulding process.

The canal's brush with Devizes is fleeting. Between Kennet Lock (50) and the Barracks site, the town's outskirts lie above and behind a deep cutting – now hidden, now flaunting long, well-kept gardens – that breaks through the natural barrier between the Avon valley and the Vale of Pewsey. One secluded stretch has an almost intimidating feel where the imagination might easily create swirling mists rising up around dank vegetation. Devizes Wharf has sufficient historic and emotional connections to ensure its place as one of pilgrimage for waterways enthusiasts. That said, the restoration and refurbishment of wharfside buildings, though admirable and aesthetically pleasing, has created a setting that exudes, for some, an antiseptic quality … perhaps that missing 'spark' can be rekindled as more craft enjoy the splendours of a restored canal.

" … near Devizes barracks, we grounded mid-stream, where the mud had silted to such an extent as to deny us even the few inches of water that we required. It took six people to pull her through the mud, with the three of us on one bank and on the other an obliging farmer and two prisoners-of-war, to whom we threw a line."

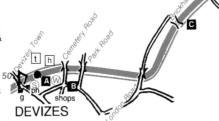

Restoration
Lock 50 (named Kennet Lock in 1982) was closed in 1951; for most of the 80s it was the only lock of the 29-lock flight fitted with top and bottom gates. Before the re-opening of the whole flight by HM Queen Elizabeth II in August 1990, Maton Lock (49) was navigable only by special dispensation. Eventually all locks on the flight will be named.

DEVIZES
Detailed information on Devizes is on p.29.

HORTON
A small, mainly agricultural, village with some distinctive half-timbered and thatched cottages. The late General Sir Hugh Stockwell, President of the K&ACT for many years, lived in the village.
Sustenance
BRIDGE INN – a friendly canal-orientated pub with good bar food; canalside by Horton Bridge.
Public Transport
ROAD – infrequent Wilts & Dorset service to/from Devizes and Pewsey; details from Salisbury (01722) 336855.

BISHOP'S CANNINGS
Another agriculturally-based hamlet, loosely arranged around the centrepiece, the church.
Sustenance
CROWN INN – home-cooked food in a traditional setting; ¾ mile north west of Bishop's Cannings Swing Bridge.

Sightseeing
ST MARY'S CHURCH – a surprisingly magnificent spired church for such a small village. Cruciform in plan, it bears an uncanny resemblance to Salisbury Cathedral – which is not surprising as it was built on what was the Bishop of Salisbury's estate. Some parts date from the 12th century.

FOR THE BOATER
Wharfside Chandlery, Couch Lane, Devizes SN10 1EB; tel: Devizes (01380) 725007. Extensive chandlery, K&A windlasses, BW keys.

Devizes Marina, Horton Avenue, Devizes SN10 2RH; tel: Devizes (01380) 730033/ 725300. Moorings, chandlery, full engineering service, boat brokerage, slipway, covered repair dock, gas, diesel, pump-out, 'Elsan' disposal, K&A windlasses, BW keys.

White Horse Boats, 8 Southgate Close, Devizes SN10 5AQ; tel: Devizes (01380) 728504. 4-6 berth hire-craft, day hire, boatbuilding and repairs, water and rubbish disposal by arrangement.

As the canal winds itself around the villages of Bishop's Cannings, Horton, Allington, All Cannings and the ever-present Knoll, its character is changing. The engineering features associated with the west and the valley of the Avon and the pastoral wanderings of the Vale of Pewsey gradually merge. Agriculture is king in a landscape where man has tilled the soil for as long as anyone can recall … only the machinery has changed, though horse-ploughing continued across these gentle pastures long after the take-over of the tractor elsewhere. As west-bound travellers will have already discovered, the Vale of Pewsey is a place of antiquity, the canal and its artefacts just another example of man leaving his mark across the heart of downland Wiltshire. At All Cannings Cross Farm the remains of a substantial Iron Age settlement were excavated in the 1920s.

Restoration
Navigation of the 15-mile Long Pound became increasingly difficult during the 50s – the more so when the pound's dredger was removed to Sharpness. Even in the 40s, one 'pleasure' cruise had found the pound to be "choked for miles with reeds". Weed clearance in the 60s by the Trust's Junior Division was followed by dredging in the early 70s after which navigation was again possible.

A Last Line of Defence?
Alongside the towpath, just south of Horton Bridge (see opposite) there is what appears to be a job-lot of tank traps – concrete megaliths of all shapes and sizes. These and numerous brick and concrete pill-boxes are a feature of the canal throughout Wiltshire and Berkshire and are, of course, relics of the Second World War when the K&A was regarded as a 'natural' anti-tank defence line. Though they were never put to the test, they remain as monuments to one of the last successful carrying operations on the canal.

B Contours and Cuttings: Like all canals, the K&A has its own 'slot' in the history of Britain's inland waterways. It is the product of the second wave of canal building, the so-called 'Canal Mania' that in the early 1790s (46 canal-related Acts of Parliament were passed between 1791 and 1794) sought to capitalise on the success of the pioneering schemes of the first Canal Age. It is thus a product also of an age of more advanced canal technology, of a time when cuttings and embankments were being increasingly used to keep the cut on the straight and narrow rather than allow it to wander too far off course. Across the Vale of Pewsey, between Devizes and Wootton Rivers, there are 15 miles of lock-free boating as, with the minimum of deviation from the winding contour below the Vale's northern scarp, the canal gently meanders, aided here and there by the occasional, if undramatic, cutting or embankment. Later canals were more ruthless in their use of what became known as 'cut and fill' techniques and all but ignored the natural contours in ensuring as direct a route as practical.

C Salisbury Avon: North of Horton, almost unnoticed, the canal cuts across a tiny stream. Tiny it might be, but it is the western beginning of the Salisbury Avon, the eastern branch of which flows through Pewsey.

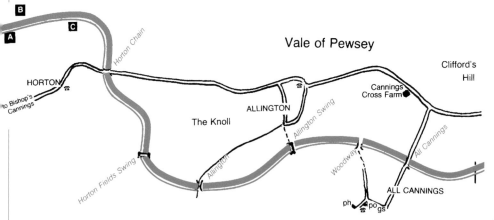

Vale of Pewsey

Clifford's Hill

Cannings Cross Farm

HORTON

to Bishop's Cannings

Horton Chain

ALLINGTON

The Knoll

Allington Swing

Allington

Horton Fields Swing

Woodway

All Cannings

ALL CANNINGS

ph   po   gs

ALLINGTON
A rural hamlet scattered east of the Knoll.

ALL CANNINGS
Yet another Vale of Pewsey village which the canal by-passes; the tall central clock tower of its largely 14th-century church oversees a large village green.

Sustenance
KING'S ARMS – bar snacks in a typical country pub; ½ mile south of Woodway and All Cannings Bridges.

Sightseeing
THE VILLAGE POND – situated at the southern end of the village, the pond is one of several in the area to lay claim to being the source of Wiltshire's 'moonraker' legend. Some 18th-century villagers, it seems, had hidden smuggled brandy kegs in the pond and were using hay rakes to retrieve them when two excisemen appeared. They quickly explained away their activities by claiming to have been trying to retrieve the large round cheese (the moon's reflection) from the water. Though the excisemen believed this explanation, they were left with a poor opinion of the Wiltshire intellect.

Public Transport
ROAD – infrequent Wilts & Dorset service to/from Devizes and Pewsey; details from Salisbury (01722) 336855.

A Barge Inn: The hamlet of Honeystreet is a product of the canal and its one hostelry, the *Barge Inn*, was an integral part of the canalside community that, from the early 19th century, served this new artery. This was no ordinary alehouse for, with its own brewhouse, bakehouse and slaughterhouse, it supplied the canal and the community with all its basic needs. The original building was destroyed by fire in 1858 but was rebuilt and back in business within six months … time enough for one of its clientele to 'decorate' a window thus: "Syd Biggs got drunk, May 2nd 1872".

B Honeystreet Wharf: The wharf at Honeystreet was owned and run by Robbins, Lane and Pinnegar who were the last regular K&A-based traders. Here too, many of the craft used on this and neighbouring navigations were built. The 'Kennet' barges of the Wey Navigation and the Basingstoke Canal originated at Honeystreet as did larger craft – as large as the locks would permit – for use on the Avon and at Bristol. The company also owned the adjacent timberyard and ran their own boat fleet to bring in wood from Avonmouth and Hungerford. An engraved stone on the forlorn chimney shaft behind the wharf records the potted history of what was originally Robbins & Co: "K&A Canal finished 1810. This Wharf commenced 1811. K&A Road made 1842. Part of Wharf burnt 1854. Rebuilt and enlarged 1855. This chimney erected 1859". It does not record that the company vacated the site in the late 1940s, defeated, despite dogged persistence, by a decaying canal.

C The Ridgeway: The canal bisects the line of the prehistoric highway east of Honeystreet, being one of the several 'broken' lengths in Wiltshire, indeed the name Honeystreet was, according to *The Place-Names of Wiltshire*, "a name given to the Ridgeway as it crosses Pewsey Vale. Probably so-called because it was a muddy road." North of Overton Hill (four miles away) the track becomes a designated long-distance footpath, continuing as such for the 89 miles to Ivinghoe Beacon in Buckinghamshire.

Almost river-like the canal cuts its circuitous course around the southern edge of Stanton St Bernard, Alton Barnes and Alton Priors. Only Honeystreet flirts with the waterway, indeed the relationship between the two was to be deep and lasting; it is perhaps difficult to imagine these reed-fringed waters as harbouring a particularly busy waterside centre. At times the vista is so open that the northern ridges of Tan Hill and Milk Hill – a white horse cut into the canal-facing slope of the latter – loom larger than life. Two of the scarp's outposts, Woodborough Hill and Picked Hill, are closer, their bare slopes marked with the evidence of prehistoric field systems (lynchets) and overseen by tree-tufted crowns. The Vale's northern ridge is traversed by Wansdyke, a defensive earth-work bisected in turn by a prehistoric highway, the Ridgeway; both feature in the circular walk on page 61.

Restoration
The Long Pound's deterioration during the 50s was due in part to the lack of access through the Devizes and Wootton Rivers flights and the subsequent falling off of boat movements until the dredging of the 70s. Research in the mid-80s demonstrated that boat movements were, not surprisingly, a major factor in weed control.

Vale of Pewsey

Woodborough Hill

Picked H

" … we reached the floating bridge at Honeystreet … with much difficulty we undid the rusty bolts and freed one end which I started to punt with the long boat-hook, but the bridge was so water-logged that when I got out mid-stream it not only started to sink, but heeled over ready to capsize at any moment."

STANTON ST BERNARD
A curious hotch-potch of a village dominated in the main by its battlemented Victorian church.

HONEYSTREET
Clearly a product of the canal; its brick cottages and wharfside warehousing untypical of the Vale of Pewsey, their allegiance being instead to the Kennet & Avon and its attendant trade.
Sustenance
BARGE INN – good food in a friendly atmosphere liberally sprinkled with canal lore; canalside between Stanton and Honeystreet Bridges.

ALTON BARNES and ALTON PRIORS
These two villages rub shoulders; together they would scarcely make a village of note, assuming, that is, that size was a criterion in such things. 'Alton' means 'the farm by the springs' and it is a small willow-lined brook that seems to be the line of demarcation between the two distinct and distinctive churches.
Sightseeing
ALTON BARNES WHITE HORSE, ST MARY'S CHURCH, WANSDYKE, THE RIDGEWAY and TAN HILL – all, and more, feature in the circular walk described on page 61.

FOR THE BOATER
Gibson's Boat Services, Old Builder's Wharf, Honeystreet SN9 5PS; tel: Marlborough (01672) 851232. Water, diesel, gas, 'Elsan' disposal, rubbish disposal, pump-out, boat surveys & deliveries, K&A windlasses, BW keys.

The town that gives this picturesque vale its name lies in a hollow, half-a-mile south of the canal, the latter preferring to cling to the winding edge of the chalk footslopes. The distinctive wharf area is necessarily a product of the canal, its buildings and adjacent cottages and hostelry clearly having an affinity with it. A different relationship with the waterway is in evidence to the west where Wilcot Wide Water and its wooded banks create a unique interlude, a secluded and peaceful place overseen by the twin sentinels of Ladies Bridge and Picked Hill. Seclusion of a quite different kind explains the distinctive suspension bridge that provides private access to the emparked classical mansion at Stowell. The house itself is not visible but then there are several delightful canalside brick and thatched cottages hereabouts.

Restoration
Although unnavigable for conventional craft between the 50s and 70s, the 15-mile Long Pound gave birth to the annual (Easter) Devizes – Westminster canoe race. The idea originated in 1948 in Pewsey, when a local gentleman offered £20 to anyone who could navigate a boat from Pewsey to Westminster in less than 100 hrs. Weed clearing and dredging in the 60s, 70s and 80s has reduced the time to around 16 hrs.

A Ladies Bridge and Wilcot Water:
The ornate façades and balustraded parapets of Ladies Bridge are reminiscent of Rennie's aqueducts in the west and as such are no idle whim but part of a 'local difficulty' encountered by the canal's engineers. It seems that Lady Wroughton, the owner of Wilcot Manor, would only allow the canal to cut through her land if the aftermath resembled an ornamental lake rather than a scar on the landscape. Thus the Wide Water and Ladies Bridge appeased the noble Lady's aesthetic sensibilities.

B Swanborough Tump:
The path south of Ladies Bridge leads to Swanborough Tump, believed to be the 'Swanborough' at which Alfred the Great, King of Wessex, wrote his will when he and his entourage were being hard-pressed by the 'heathen' Danes.

C Bristol & Salisbury Canal:
The early 1790s spawned many canal schemes which, had they all come to fruition, would have created a Fen-like terrain south of the Thames. One such project, the Bristol & Salisbury Canal, would have linked the projected Salisbury & Southampton Canal with the K&A at Wilcot while another cut would have linked the Andover Canal with Pewsey.

D Pewsey Wharf:
In 1984 the wharf here hosted the first ever National Trailboat Rally and, predictably, the rain fell. Rain no doubt fell frequently on the so-called 'navvies' (short for 'navigators') who built the canal and, contrary to popular belief, these were not all of the rough-and-ready Irish variety. Here, at Pewsey Wharf, local tradition has it that French prisoner-of-wars worked on the canal and, at the end of the day, were summoned back to their prison by the sounding of a horn … hence the uncanal-like name of the local pub.

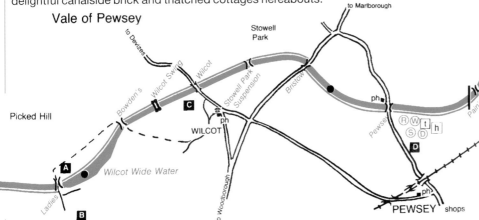

Vale of Pewsey

to Marlborough

Stowell Park

to Devizes

Bowden's
Wilcot Swing
Wilcot
Stowell Park Suspension
Bristol
Pain's

Picked Hill

C

ph
WILCOT

ph

A
Wilcot Wide Water

Ladies

B

to Woodborough

PEWSEY shops

FOR THE BOATER
Some swing bridges can only be unlocked with a windlass.

Cherry Craft, Glebe Cottage, High Street, Shrewton, Salisbury SP3 4DD; tel: Shrewton (01980) 620960. Boat hire, moorings; by Ladies Bridge.

WILCOT
Clustering amiably around its triangular green, Wilcot exudes a sleepy Wiltshire charm that is as deep and warming as the rooftop thatches.
Sustenance
GOLDEN SWAN – excellent home-cooked food served in homely village surroundings; also B&B; ¼ mile south-east of Wilcot green.

PEWSEY
Canalside Pewsey is a product of the canal; the town itself lies ½ mile away to the south. Pewsey is the capital of the Vale, still, in a sense, the 'little island' that its ancient name, 'Pevisige', implies. Its river is the (Salisbury) Avon and its three radiating roads are policed by a statue of King Alfred, a reminder that this area was once the domain of Saxon Kings.
Sustenance
FRENCH HORN – good food always available, with daily specials; canalside by Pewsey Bridge.

There are seven other pubs in Pewsey; these are, in order of proximity to the canal: CROWN, ROYAL OAK, GREYHOUND, PHOENIX, MOONRAKERS, ALFRED'S, and COOPER'S ARMS.
Shops
All the basics plus Lloyd's Bank.
Sightseeing
PEWSEY WHITE HORSE – this hillside horse, about a mile south of the town below the Everleigh road, is, arguably, the most splendidly proportioned of all the Wiltshire hill figures. It was cut in 1937 to commemorate the coronation of George VI but is said to supersede an earlier, 18th-century horse, complete with rider.
Public Transport
RAIL – frequent services on the main London to the South-West line; details from 0345 484950.
ROAD – local and Marlborough, Salisbury and Devizes services with Wilts & Dorset; details from Salisbury (01722) 336855.

A Mileposts: Canal Companies were required by law to erect mileposts, an essential basis for calculating tolls. Styles and materials varied from one canal to another and sometimes even along the same canal, while some, like road-side milestones, gave distances to and from two locations. On the K&A, mileages were recorded from Kennet Mouth at Reading (though, curiously, locks were numbered from Hanham) with the 'quarters' indicated in Roman numerals – I, II and III.

B New Mill Wharf: Little remains of the small wharf west of New Mill Bridge; even the adjacent hostelry, the *Liddiard Arms*, has gone.

C The Long Pound: Few canals manage to maintain a lock-free level for as long as 15 miles … by the same token few can claim 29 locks in a little over two miles such as at Devizes. The K&A maintains its level here by judiciously following the winding contour that represents the division between the chalk slopes and Pewsey Vale and its greensand bottom … aided and abetted by short cuttings and embankments, often barely perceptible as such.

D Wootton Rivers Locks: As at Wilcot (see page 33), the owners of the land through which the canal was cut at Wootton Rivers, St John's College, Cambridge, made certain stipulations regarding two of the bridges over the waterway. These, it seems, had to be 'carriage bridges' – crossings not only capable of accommodating the horse-drawn vehicles of the day but also with the minimum of incline on their approaches.

Travelling east, locks are back in fashion with the Wootton Rivers flight while travelling west, peace and quiet is suddenly a novelty as the main London-West Country line ends its 30-mile flirtation with the canal. This is the eastern extent of the Vale of Pewsey with the navigation weaving its almost secret way to and from the four stepping stones that separate the Vale from the summit level. Rich rolling farmland, punctuated by occasional flurries of trees, falls gently down to the water's edge as it drifts through low cuttings and embankments under the ever-present scrutiny of Martinsell Hill to the north. The stream that wriggles its way between canal and railway is one of the eastern branches of the Avon … no, not *that* Avon, but a lesser flow that wends its way to the south coast via Salisbury.

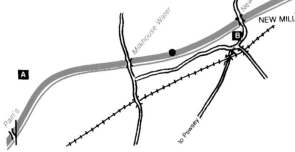

Vale of Pewsey

WOOTTON RIVERS

CUCKOO'S KNOB

NEW MILL

NEW MILL
This scattered canalside hamlet lost the mill that gave it its name to residential usage some years back; gone too is the pub, the *Liddiard Arms, t*hat once satisfied many a boatman's thirst.

WOOTTON RIVERS
Like many Vale of Pewsey villages, Wootton Rivers is based on a single street. As such it is typical, but its numerous timber-framed and thatched cottages and houses set it apart and create a feeling of mellow harmony.
Sustenance
ROYAL OAK – attractive, 16th-century village pub with B&B and good food; 1/4 mile north of Wootton Rivers Bridge.
Sightseeing
ST ANDREW'S CHURCH CLOCK – despite the obvious – letters instead of numbers – the clock here is more than meets the eye. It was meticulously put together by a local enthusiast, Jack Spratt, from countless unlikely contributions from the villagers – chaff-cutters, pipes, reaping-machines, bedsteads et al –

to commemorate the coronation of 1911. Its chime is as unusual as the sum of its parts for, in 6-hourly cycles, it emits a different chime every quarter of an hour.
Public Transport
ROAD – infrequent Wilts & Dorset service between Burbage and Pewsey; details from Salisbury (01722) 336855.

Restoration
The Wootton Rivers locks fell into disrepair during the 50s and were restored – the first in Wiltshire – and re-opened in 1973. The re-opening of the Wootton Rivers flight established, between Crofton Top Lock (55) and Devizes, 18 1/2 miles of cruising – a significant part of the 27 locks and 41 miles restored by 1975.

FOR THE BOATER

Remember to SLOW DOWN when passing FISHERMEN

A BREAKING WASH damages the BANKS

It doesn't feel any different being on a canal's summit level. At 450ft above sea level, the short 2½-mile stretch between Cadley (54) and Croft Top (55) locks is the canal's highest point … whichever way you go it can only be downhill. Hereabouts walkers, it must be said, are a cut above the rest for they have their own private summit atop the towpath-less Bruce Tunnel. And though the boater has firsthand experience of the canal's only tunnel, there is the small problem of coping with emerging to find that the railway has swapped sides. But the rest is shared: the cuttings either side of the tunnel, the rolling farmland, the open parkland and the locks. South of Brimslade Lock (53) stands what appears to be just another farmhouse … but be not deceived, for both house and ancient oaks share a more illustrious heritage dating back to the 16th century.

Restoration
Having fallen into disrepair during the 50s, the Wootton Rivers flight (51-54) was restored to navigation in 1973. Bath, Semington and Seend flights were also restored during the 70s but, unlike Wootton Rivers, suffered the indignity of remaining unused until the problems of water supply and maintenance agreements were sorted out. Bruce Tunnel never required restoration as such but was inaccessible for many years.

A Burbage Wharf: The tastefully-restored buildings that form the backdrop to Burbage Wharf and its replica crane date back to the early 19th century when the then owner of Savernake Forest, the Earl of Ailesbury, had the wharf built. Constructed of Bath stone and local bricks – the latter each marked with an 'A' – the wharf was the nearest point on the canal to Marlborough which never got its proposed direct canal link. The wooden crane is an exact replica of an original which, because of its dangerous state, had to be removed in 1971. Large stones weighing over two tons give stability to the centre post.

B Burbage Bridge: As at Mill Bridge near Great Bedwyn (see page 36), the underside of Burbage Bridge shows evidence of early attempts to construct a 'skew' bridge by using wedge-shaped blocks of stone. John Rennie was one of the first canal engineers to come to grips with the problem of crossing existing roads at an angle. Eventually the skills evolved, and became almost commonplace, in time to facilitate the spectacular viaducts of the Railway Age.

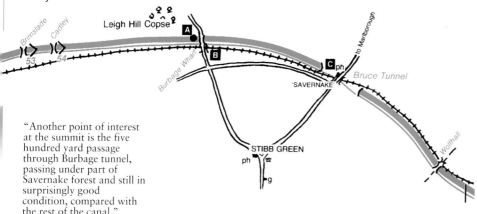

"Another point of interest at the summit is the five hundred yard passage through Burbage tunnel, passing under part of Savernake forest and still in surprisingly good condition, compared with the rest of the canal."

C Bruce Tunnel: Deep cuttings either side of Bruce Tunnel, and the fact that the hill it pierces is fairly low, raise the question of the need for the 502yd bore in the first place. It was Thomas Bruce, Earl of Ailesbury, whose land it traversed, who insisted that it be built. Rennie's original plan had been to bore a longer tunnel at a lower and more southerly level, but the cost was prohibitive. Bruce Tunnel boasts the second largest cross-section of Britain's remaining navigable tunnels; it is brick-lined throughout (bricks came from the Canal Company's brickworks alongside the Caen Hill locks – see page 27). There being no towpath, horses crossed above while boatmen pulled themselves and their craft through by means of a chain hung along the wall. A stone tablet above the eastern portal, dated 1810, recognizes the part played by Thomas Bruce while a similar tablet at the other end remains blank.

STIBB GREEN
A cluster of undefined habitations that seems to have escaped from Burbage … perhaps the road junction is its *raison d'être*.
Sustenance
THREE HORSESHOES – good bar food; less than a mile south from Burbage Wharf Bridge.

'SAVERNAKE'
There is no longer such a place though at one time a small community did lay claim to the area atop the tunnel; it remains a convenient label for the area between Brimslade and Bruce.
Sightseeing
SAVERNAKE FOREST – 2,300 acres of woodland with eight 'Walks' radiating geometrically from the centre. As well as many picnic sights, it includes – in the south-east corner – a classical monument erected by the Earl of Ailesbury to commemorate George III's supposed recovery from madness! Best access from the canal is about a mile north from Burbage Wharf Bridge.
BRIMSLADE FARM – Originally the country seat of Sir Edward Ernle, which the canal effectively severed. His many-gabled, essentially Elizabethan home remains as Brimslade Farm to the south of Brimslade Lock (53).
WOLFHALL – The red-brick house that stands in a dip opposite today's Wolfhall is Tudor in origin as evidenced by its tall polygonal chimney stacks. Here it was that Henry VIII met Jane Seymour whom he later married.
Public Transport
ROAD – infrequent services between Pewsey and Marlborough along the A346 and over the tunnel; details from Salisbury (01722) 336855.

A Crofton Leat: On the offside above Crofton Top Lock (55) a small channel enters the canal. Crofton leat was cut to bring water from Wilton Water via Crofton Pumping Station to the canal's summit pound whence it would fall through 52 locks and 35 miles to Reading and 37 locks and 38 miles to Bath. Maintaining sufficient water levels in the short (2½-mile) summit was – and still is – important with every boat that passes through taking with it a lock-full of water.

B Crofton Pumping Station: Crofton began life as a compromise. A lower and longer 18-mile summit level incorporating a longer tunnel was the original plan but the cost was prohibitive, thus the need for pumps to raise Wilton's water 40ft up to a higher summit. The same two steam engines worked from 1812 until 1959 when the shortening of the pump-house chimney by 30ft resulted in insufficient draught. The Crofton Society has lovingly restored both pumps and since 1970, when it was re-opened by Sir John Betjeman, Crofton Pumping Station and its 'steaming' weekends have proved a popular attraction.The chimney was restored to its full height in 1997.

C Wilton Water: The lake at Wilton was artificially created by damming a narrow branching valley – hence its curious shape – and is fed by natural springs. Today it still feeds the canal but doubles as a fascinating haven for wildlife where numerous species of waterfowl, from the common mallard to the rarer pochard, can be seen.

D Mill Bridge: It seems fitting that here, where early attempts at 'skewing' a bridge (see page 35) are in evidence, should have been the home of Benjamin Lloyd, the stonemason who worked on Bruce Tunnel. His house still stands between railway and road, the stone for it and other local works having been unloaded on the wharf, south-east of the bridge.

E Great Bedwyn Wharf: Now a car park, the large wharf area used to boast two coal merchants – mind you, before the 1832 Reform Bill, this was a so-called 'rotten borough' with *two* members of Parliament.

This is a busy stretch of waterway with locks aplenty and the robust brick of Crofton Pumping Station to fire the imagination. Crofton is, of course, directly connected with the more natural environment of Wilton Water to the south for together they feed water to the canal's summit level above Crofton Top Lock (55). The whole area is similarly one of contrasts from the ragged abutments of the three lines that once carried the Midland & South Western Junction Railway across the canal at the top of the Crofton locks to the three pheasant-infested hillside copses north-east of Wilton Water; from the hill-top splendour of the restored Wilton Windmill to images of a Saxon battle fought in 675. All but the railway remnants feature in the walk on page 62 … a Roman road is thrown in by way of compensation!

Restoration
The chimney stack of Crofton Pumping Station was lowered in 1959 which effectively curtailed further pumping; the station was bought by the Trust in 1968 and re-opened by the Crofton Society in 1971. All locks (55-65) became unusable in the 50s, navigable access to Crofton via locks 61-65 being re-established in 1981; the remaining six locks of the Crofton flight (55-60) were opened to navigation in the spring of 1989.

CROFTON
The hamlet of Crofton is scattered north of the canal where it severs the old Roman road.
Sightseeing
CROFTON PUMPING STATION – Static displays daily, April-October; also 'steaming' weekends once a month. Details from Marlborough (01672) 870300.

WILTON
A small, attractive village memorable for its thatched cottages and duck pond.
Sustenance
SWAN INN – good food in warming village inn; ½ mile south of Lock 60.
Sightseeing
WILTON WINDMILL – open summer Sunday afternoons and bank holidays; tel: Marlborough (01672) 870268 for details.
WILTON WATER is featured (along with the Windmill and Crofton) in more detail in the walk described on page 62.

GREAT BEDWYN
A 'rotten' borough in its time but today it exudes an innocence that belies a past stretching back beyond the Romans. Its mellow brick, flint and thatch seem content with the new order of things.
Sustenance
CROSS KEYS – bar snacks and B&B; 200 yds west of Bedwyn Wharf Bridge.
THREE TUNS – hot and cold bar meals; ¼ mile west of Bedwyn Wharf Bridge.
Sightseeing
GREAT BEDWYN STONE MUSEUM – Visitors welcome during normal working hours; tel: Marlborough (01672) 870234 (the museum features in the walk on page 62).
Public Transport
RAIL – Great Bedwyn is on the main London to the South-West line; details on 0345 484950.
ROAD – Newbury Buses services to Marlborough and Hungerford; details from Newbury (01635) 40743. Wilts & Dorset services between Pewsey and Marlborough; details from Salisbury (01722) 336855.

FOR THE BOATER
The Bruce Charitable Trust, PO Box 21, Hungerford RG17 9YY; tel: Hungerford (01672) 515498. 12-berth, wide-beam hire-craft equipped for the disabled; based at Great Bedwyn and Foxhanger Wharf.

Remember to SLOW DOWN when passing FISHERMEN

If you are making a WASH you are going TOO FAST

Southern Boat Services, 6 Church Street, Little Bedwyn, Marlborough SN8 3JQ; tel: (01672) 870158. Water, pump-out (Saturdays by appointment only), 'Elsan' disposal, rubbish disposal, moorings, surveys (including BW Certificate of Compliance).

Restoration

Like most of the navigation between Newbury and Crofton, this section fell into disrepair during the 50s, the locks in particular suffering the indignities of time. The length from Hungerford west to Little Bedwyn was re-opened to navigation in 1977 – a plaque at Oakhill Down Lock (68) commemorates the event and acknowledges the Provincial Insurance's financial support.

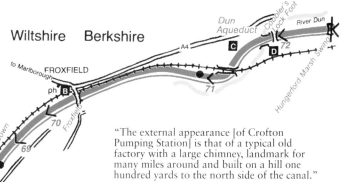

Wiltshire   Berkshire

"The external appearance [of Crofton Pumping Station] is that of a typical old factory with a large chimney, landmark for many miles around and built on a hill one hundred yards to the north side of the canal."

Despite the proximity of the railway and, east of Froxfield, the A4 trunk road, the canal manages to maintain an air of insularity. There is a peace and solitude that, the intrusion of Froxfield, Little Bedwyn and the locks notwithstanding, is both exhilarating and primordial. The docile Dun, the flurries of woodland and the open pastureland punctuated with lone trees are now at one with the cut that once scarred this landscape with its impetuosity. The Dun is crossed twice; once, almost unnoticed, in the shadow of Oak Hill and again via a low brick aqueduct. Though a modern replacement, Froxfield Bridge, the Wiltshire-Berkshire county border, is worthy of notice; by using traditional methods and materials, Planning Man rekindles here a confidence in his ability to 'listen to' the environment.

FOR THE BOATER

Some swing bridges can only be unlocked with a windlass.

Crews of boats longer than 30ft must open the swing bridge at Hungerford Marsh Lock before locking up.

LITTLE BEDWYN
Both canal and railway effectively bisect the village into its two distinct constituents – Victorian estate housing to the west and the older farming community to the east.
Sustenance
HARROW INN – bar snacks in individual, village local. 300 yds south-east of Little Bedwyn Bridge.

FROXFIELD
The village – first and last in Wiltshire – is claimed by the A4 and, with two exceptions, offers little other than traffic to the canal traveller.
Sustenance
PELICAN INN – extensive, modernised, roadside hotel, specialising in Anglo-French cuisine; on the A4, ¼ mile north-west of Froxfield Bridge.

Sightseeing
SOMERSET HOSPITAL – despite bordering the A4, this attractive group of red-brick almshouses built round regular lawns and a chapel, 'founded and endowed (in 1694) … for twenty clergy and thirty lay widows', is worth the risk. LITTLECOTE HOUSE – a Tudor-built, red-brick, stone and flint mansion, reputedly the finest in Wiltshire. Here William of Orange dined, Charles II was entertained, Elizabeth I slept … and a 16th-century baby was murdered; besides which the Romans left the fine Orpheus mosaic and the young river Kennet flows through the lush gardens. Now a hotel but open to the public on Wednesday and Sunday, Easter to end October. Tel: (01488) 682509. Less than 2 miles north from Froxfield.
Public Transport
ROAD – Newbury Buses service between Marlborough and Hungerford; details from Newbury (01635) 40743.

A Little Bedwyn's Bridges:
Two bridges cross the canal to unite the two halves of Little Bedwyn. The higher, trough-like road bridge contrasts sharply with the lower foot bridge which clearly began life as a swing bridge, until, that is, the arrival of the railway.

B Froxfield Wharf and Feeder:
Although much of the original wharf at Froxfield lies in the shadow of the nearby railway, the feeling of what used to be lingers in the air. Between the wharf and bridge the Froxfield Feeder enters the canal via a curious circular weir; it is so devised that one third of the stream enters the canal while the rest is culverted underneath. This arrangement has its origins in the need to maintain sufficient water supply to the former Oakhill Mill.

C Barrackfield Swing Bridge:
Originally there was an accommodation bridge here just east of the railway crossing. It is no more, though its 'disappearance' is destined to be more permanent than its last vanishing trick – the American Army, based locally during the last war, 'borrowed' it to use as a temporary saluting platform.

D Dun Aqueduct:
Looked at in terms of the spectacular stone aqueducts at Dundas and Avoncliff to the west, Dun Aqueduct is clearly not in the same league. That is not to say that this squat 3-arched aqueduct has no charm; the setting by Cobbler's Lock (72) and its attendant cottages is especially attractive.

A Hungerford Marsh Lock: The lock (73) is not only unique in K&A terms but it is a rarity on Britain's inland waterway network – it has a swing bridge across the lock chamber. No track or road leading to or from the bridge is immediately obvious but there is a 'right of way' that dates back to the commoners rights granted by John of Gaunt over Freeman's Marsh ... the fact that a lock ended up bang in the middle made not the slightest difference!

B St Lawrence's Church: Many old prints of the canalside St Lawrence's Church depict a building with a fascinating blend of angles. Sadly this collapsed under a massive snowfall in 1814 but was replaced by 1816 with stone brought from Bath along the newly-opened canal.

C Hungerford Wharf: It was in late 1798 that a barge carrying several casks of Russian tallow arrived at Hungerford Wharf from Newbury, the first commercial cargo to take advantage of the newly-completed link with the Thames. Nearly two centuries on, the wharf is a place of memories; gone is the crane and the gauging station, though some wharfside buildings, tastefully restored for residential use, remain. The local firm of Woodridge & Son left the site in 1962, having been contracted by the GWR to maintain the eastern end of the canal from Wootton Rivers to Reading between 1851 and 1863. An intended branch line to Marlborough from Hungerford was, like other such schemes, shelved. The Dun Feeder enters the canal here between wharf and lock.

D Dun and Denford Mills: Mill owners on the river Kennet claimed rights to its water supply long before the canal cut its parallel swathe along the river valley: Hence it was important that the Kennet & Avon Canal Act was seen to safeguard the rights of water-powered mills such as those that still stand by the confluence of the Dun and Kennet. With their livelihoods assured, mill owners understandably took full advantage of the convenient artery on their doorstep.

It is at Hungerford that the river Kennet makes its first – or final – mark on the landscape. The confluence of the rivers Dun and Kennet is at Dun Mill, one of those memorable, almost idyllic places, where the combination of tumbling waters and old buildings feeds off the natural beauty of the setting. The terrain generally is much influenced by the nearby rivers, and the channels and hatches that they once spawned to feed the old water meadows to the north and east of Hungerford. In Elizabethan times the Kennet here yielded a great amount of fish "especiallie trowtes and crevices" (a kind of crayfish), a fact that hasn't gone unnoticed at the local trout farm. Either side of the town, at Freeman's Marsh and Port Common, the land is common, the rights of the townsfolk dating far back into the mists of time.

Restoration
Derelict and decaying since the 50s, the section east of Hungerford (to Kintbury) was re-opened in 1974 while the first passage west of the town in over a quarter of a century was made in 1977. Since 1967 the navigation between Bath and Hamstead had been designated 'remainder' waterway and British Waterways had a statutory obligation only to maintain it to its condition at that time.

"No boat, as far as I could gather, had passed right through [the canal] since 1937, and it appeared doubtful that any other would do so for some time to come unless it was a canoe or something similar which could be easily carried past the locks."

HUNGERFORD

HUNGERFORD
Hungerford lies just west of the confluence of the rivers Dun and Kennet on what was once the eastern extremity of Savernake Forest. Its broad main street used to host a weekly market and three annual fairs, overseen by buildings from all post-medieval periods, though today those dating from the 18th and 19th centuries predominate. Hungerford is best known for its Hocktide ceremonies which take place on the second Tuesday after Easter. A horn summons the 99 burgesses to the Town Hall and two 'Tutti-men' are appointed who, carrying the symbols of their office, visit every house enjoying Common rights to collect a 'headpenny' and receive a kiss from the ladies of the house in exchange for an orange. At the luncheon afterwards all new commoners (known as 'colts') are formally 'shod'.
Sustenance
JOHN O'GAUNT – bar food and B&B in 17th-century surroundings; 100 yds north of Hungerford Bridge.

THREE SWANS HOTEL – snacks; restaurant and bars open to non-residents in old manor house; 200 yds south of Hungerford Bridge.
BEAR HOTEL – excellent up-market cuisine and B&B in this old, partially 13th-century, roadside inn; 200 yds north of Hungerford Bridge.
PLUME – good basic menu in local atmosphere; 200 yds south of Hungerford Bridge.
Shops
Known nationally as an antique centre; all major banks except Midland.
Sightseeing
IRON FOOT BRIDGES – the cutting of the canal necessitated new front doors for the houses either side of Hungerford Bridge, hence the iron footbridges to their new front doors at first floor level.
Public Transport
RAIL – on the main London to the South-West line; details on 0345 484950.
ROAD – Newbury Buses service to and from Newbury; details from Newbury (01635) 40743.

FOR THE BOATER
Crews of boats longer than 30ft must open the swing bridge at Hungerford Marsh Lock before locking up.

On an island between the river Kennet and the canal on the northern edge of Kintbury, stands the *Dundas Arms*, named, like Rennie's magnificent aqueduct at Limpley Stoke, after Charles Dundas, Baron Amesbury, who formally opened the canal in 1810. The hilltop village which takes its name from the river, only just touches the canal … not that anything could detract from the gloriously wooded hillocks, particularly The Wilderness and Irish Hill, that cascade down to the water's edge. South of the cut the aspect west of Kintbury is rather different with watercress beds filling the low-lying land. Opposite, feeding on the two branches of the Kennet, are water-meadows and, piercing the wooded backdrop, the cross-topped apex of the Norman Avington Church while lone, but not lonely, is the tree-sheltered chamber of Brunsden's Lock (77).

Restoration
All the locks suffered from the lack of use generated by the closures of the 50s until 1972, when those west of Kintbury were re-opened; passage through to Hungerfod was subsequently restored by 1974. The navigation east from Hamstead Lock (81) – as far as Bull's Lock (88) – was, from 1967, given 'cruiseway' status and as such BW was obliged to maintain it to a satisfactory cruising standard.

A Watercress Beds: The low-lying ground south of the canal here once boasted extensive watercress beds. For generations the 'secret' of watercress cultivation has been jealously guarded, rival growers being all too aware that Berkshire cress was much sought-after in the London markets. There was a time when cress from these beds was punted down the canal to Kintbury from where it was speedily dispatched to the capital.

B Brunsden's Lock: For a time both this lock (77) and Wire Lock (76) to the west shared the same name – Fowler's Lock. Presumably all three appellations have associations with people as none appears to have any connection with local landmarks.

C Kintbury Wharf: It was perhaps fitting that it should have been in Charles Dundas' home territory that the first section of the K&A was officially opened. On 12th June 1797 a 60-ton barge, its sole cargo the band of the 15th Regiment of Dragoons, made the 6-mile trip in festive mood from Newbury to Kintbury in 2¹/₂ hours. Dundas (the first chairman of the Canal Company) and his Committee were there to greet band and barge, to extend the hand of officialdom and to embark on the return trip which, for some reason, took an extra hour! Today Kintbury Wharf is almost a picturesque backwater but a mere century ago it was transhipping iron and coke from South Wales to five local iron works which specialized in manufacture of agricultural machinery and implements. Raw materials for the local brewery and flour mill were also brought by water while locally-produced whiting was 'exported' to Bristol.

D Whiting: This is chalk country … it is therefore not surprising that this natural local resource soon found an outlet. That outlet was the manufacture of whiting, a fine powder used in paint manufacture for which the Kintbury area, with five mills, became renowned. Between the western footslopes of Irish Hill and the canal, hidden in the ever-advancing undergrowth, lie some of the derelict and decaying remains of the last of the local whiting mills. From the nearby hill the soft upper chalk was 'farmed', broken up and sieved to remove flints, soaked in water and allowed to settle, the slurry run off and dried and the resulting whiting sent to Bristol's paint manufacturers.

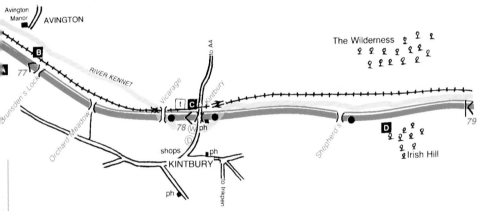

The Wilderness

Avington Manor — AVINGTON

RIVER KENNET

Brunsden's Lock — 77

to A4

Vicarage

Kintbury

C — 78 (W) ph — shops — ph — KINTBURY

ph — to Inkpen

Shepherd's Lock

D — Irish Hill

79

FOR THE BOATER

If you are making a WASH you are going TOO FAST

All craft using the river Kennet should carry an anchor.

AVINGTON
The ancient village of Avington manages to retain an almost 'other world' quality despite the proximity of the A4.
Sightseeing
AVINGTON CHURCH – This tiny, rectangular church, aisleless and towerless, is almost entirely Norman; contains a cylindrical stone font and a delightful chancel arch.

KINTBURY
Several roads converged at Kintbury, the main village being south of the navigation. The erstwhile brick, tanning, wool dyeing, silk-weaving and whiting industries have conceded defeat to agriculture.
Sustenance
DUNDAS ARMS HOTEL – large hostelry with restaurant; navigation-side by Kintbury Bridge.
PRINCE OF WALES – good food in friendly village local; 300 yds south-east of navigation.
BLUE BALL – lunch-time snacks in top-of-village local; ¹/₄ mile south of navigation.
Public Transport
RAIL – regular services on the London to South-West line; details on 0345 484950.
ROAD – Newbury Buses service to and from Newbury; details from Newbury (01635) 40743.

A River Kennet: The Kennet & Avon can be divided into three quite distinctive types of navigation: river (as from Bristol to Bath); canal (as from Bath to Kintbury); and canalised river (Kintbury to Reading). East of Newbury, with the Kennet fast-approaching its rendezvous with Mother Thames, the river is increasingly wider and deeper and, save where it takes to wandering, its influence correspondingly greater. On the other hand, east of Copse Lock (80) it is a younger Kennet that mingles with the man-made cut.

B Benham Broad: Alliteration notwithstanding, Wilcot Wide Water (see page 33) and Benham Broad are products of similar fetishes, though the latter is aided and abetted by several backwaters of the river Kennet. The fetish in question was, in this case, the desire of one of the canal's promoters, Lord Craven, to ensure that where the navigation passed through his estate of Benham Park it should have an additional aesthetic quality. Thus the Broad's origins are artificial though few would deny its legacy of natural attributes.

C Pickletimber Railway Bridge: The main London-West Country line and the canal part company through Newbury and its suburbs; though out of earshot, they are never more than ⅓ mile apart. The western reunification/separation is at Pickletimber Railway Bridge, so-called after an earlier wooden trestle structure.

East-bound travellers will become more aware of the influence of the river Kennet as more and more of it infiltrates the navigation. Those heading west may perhaps see things differently with the river less and less a factor and the man-made alternative in the ascendancy. But from whatever aspect no one can fail to notice, even extol, the beauty of this bosky vale as the waters, man-made and natural, flirt with the splendour of More Wood, Hamstead Park, Benham Park, Enborne Copse and their sporadic, but equally memorable, outriders. The locks nestle like black and white gems in a green setting, many overseen by the weathered stone of their attendant bridges. You will pass this way with a sense of wonder … and not just with fertile speculation on why Pickletimber Railway Bridge is so-called!

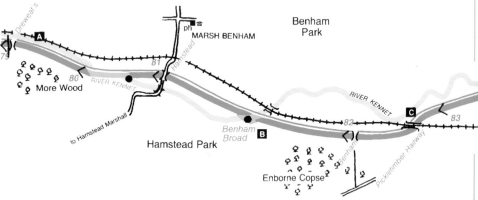

Restoration
Decaying since the 50s, Copse Lock (80) was restored in 1972. Higg's (83), Benham (82) and Hamstead (81) went out of action in 1952 with the result that John Gould's carrying business was effectively 'land-locked' at Newbury. Hamstead Lock was restored in 1971 – the first west of Newbury – with work completed on Benham and Higg's shortly afterwards to allow through navigation to Kintbury.

MARSH BENHAM
A crossroad of scattered habitation, the former, thatched pub seemingly the hub.
Sustenance
WATER RAT – good food in the old pub, now a restaurant with bar; ¼ mile north and east of Hamstead Bridge.
Sightseeing
ICICLE BALLOON MEETING – Marsh

Benham is the site of this annual(Hot Air Balloon) event (1st weekend in January). HAMSTEAD PARK and ST MARY'S CHURCH both feature in the circular walk described on page 63.
Public Transport
ROAD – Newbury Buses services between Hungerford and Newbury; details from Newbury (01635) 40743.

FOR THE BOATER
Boaters should be aware of the influence of the river Kennet's current, especially where it leaves or joins a man-made section of the navigation.

All craft using the river Kennet should carry an anchor.

Newbury dominates the navigation's course for a little over a mile. River and cut alternate as their waters mingle with the ever-present, though never overbearing, backdrop of this attractive town. Waterside Newbury is thus a delightful interlude, with the elegant span of Town Bridge the unforeseen link between the old Kennet Navigation and the newer canal to Bath. East of the town the Kennet's backwaters begat mills at Greenham and Ham while the waters of the river Lambourn enter an unnavigable section to the north. Westwards the scene is characteristically canal-like with a long straight cut punctuated by the defunct railway crossing of the old Lambourn Valley Railway and what were once called First Lock (now Guyer's, 84) and First Bridge (now Enborne); here it was, in October 1794, that excavation westwards first began.

Restoration
Being one of the few parts of the navigation to be 'worked' since the 50s, it is hardly surprising that Guyer's (84) and Newbury (85) needed no major refurbishment. Greenham (86) fell into disrepair in 1971 and was rebuilt in 1972; that same year Ham (87) became unsafe and remained unworkable until rebuilt in 1981 by which time Greenham was causing problems. Navigation through to Bull's (88) was re-established in 1983.

A West Mills Wharf: The picturesque setting around West Mills Swing Bridge belies its manufacturing and trading heritage. The cottages to the south-west began life as a weaving factory which in turn housed some of the so-called 'navvies' working on the canal. West Mills Wharf is on the other side of the bridge, the site today more evocative of its past through its atmosphere than any tangible remains. Here it was in 1950 that John Knill made his first – and last – delivery of salt from Middlewich; his enterprise was overcome by a decaying canal. At the western end of the swing bridge stood West Mills itself, its surviving silo having been converted to flats. Until developers stepped in during the 1970s, Town Mill occupied a site between the canal and St Nicholas' Church.

B Newbury Lock: Newbury Lock was the first completed on the new canal in 1796. It is the only lock fitted with lever-operated ground-paddles of a kind common on northern canals, known as jack or side cloughs.

C Town Bridge: Being the limit of navigation of the original Kennet Navigation (see page 4), Newbury's elegant Town Bridge never had a towpath. With the cutting of the canal west-wards, horse-drawn craft thus had a problem, particularly as it was forbidden – as enforced by the notice on the lock-keeper's cottages – for horses to haul *across* the main road. The difficulty of navigating upstream was solved by a special float located at the cottage; with the barge tied up below the bridge and the horse to the far side, the float was attached to the tow-rope and allowed to drift downstream, under the bridge, to the barge. Working downstream was easier with assistance from the horse's initial momentum out of the lock and the natural flow.

D Newbury Wharf: A car park and the new A34 have obliterated much of what was one of the busiest wharves on the navigation. Originally, of course, it was the terminal wharf of the Kennet Navigation and as such became a busy transhipment depot with wharves and warehousing surrounding a large basin. The former Granary, now the town's Museum, remains as the most substantial survivor of the basin complex. Another wharf, Greenham, where the large 'Newbury' barges were built, lies downstream under the Court House and Police Station.

E Greenham Mill: The strange events of 25 June 1811 in which Greenham Mill played a part, speak for themselves on page 44.

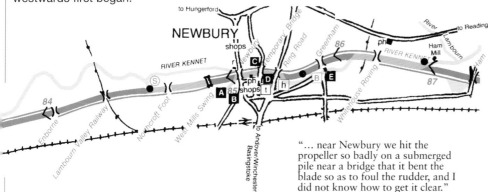

to Hungerford
NEWBURY
shops
to Reading
RIVER KENNET
River Lambourn
Ham Mill
RIVER KENNET
84
Enborne
Lambourn Valley Railway
Northcroft Foot
West Mills Swing
Newbury Swing Bridge
Temporary Bridge
Ring Road
Greenham
86
to Andover/Winchester/Basingstoke
Whitehouse Roving Bridge
87
85
shops
Ham

"... near Newbury we hit the propeller so badly on a submerged pile near a bridge that it bent the blade so as to foul the rudder, and I did not know how to get it clear."

FOR THE BOATER
Some swing bridges can only be unlocked with a windlass.

Newbury Lock (85) has unique ground paddles called 'cloughs'; to fill the lock the long lever should be raised to the upright position and lowered again when the lock is full.

Below Newbury Lock (85), the river Kennet and a mill stream enter the channel from opposite sides; in fast-flowing conditions boaters – particularly those cruising east – should not underestimate the effect of the current at this point.

Newbury Boat Company, Greenham Lock Cottage, London Road, Newbury RG14 5SN; tel: Newbury (01635) 42884. Water, 'Elsan' disposal, pump-out, diesel, gas, slipway, dry dock, covered paint dock, cranage, moorings, K&A windlasses, BW keys and licences; boat & engine repairs by arrangement.

NEWBURY
Newbury is dealt with in greater detail on page 44; canalside facilities only are detailed below.
Sustenance
LOCK STOCK & BARREL – popular pub serving day-time bar meals; by Newbury Bridge.

OLD WAGGON AND HORSES – bar snacks; backs onto the river east of Newbury Bridge; entrance from Mansion House Street.
WHITE HOUSE – good food in road-side inn with strong river connections; backs onto the river by Whitehouse Bridge.

A Swing Bridges: The Modern Ham Bridge replaces an original swing bridge as does the smart new Bull's Swing Bridge. Swing bridges on the Kennet & Avon are not only a feature of it but also play an important part in the technological history of such 'movable' bridges. John Rennie was an innovator and when faced with the problem of so many such crossings on the K&A, sought to make it easier for the hitherto cumbersome wooden bridges to be swung. Thus did the ball-bearing come to the rescue, with Rennie the first engineer to put this embryonic technology to such practical use. The argument as to whether or not he 'invented' the ball-bearing specifically for the canal's swing bridges remains insoluble, though their use certainly predates the *Dictionary of National Biography*'s claim that Robert Stevenson used them first, for cranes in Bell Rock Lighthouse. That said, the Kennet Navigation is, of course, older than Rennie's canal … imagine what a relief it must have been to local boatmen when everything began to run that bit more smoothly.

B Bull's Lock: This was the first – and last – lock to be restored by volunteer labour from the Kennet & Avon Canal Trust under the supervision of BW.

C Monkey Marsh Lock: Locks on the Kennet Navigation were originally turf-sided. These were constructed of timber to about 2ft above the lock's lower level, above which their turfed sides sloped away at an angle of about 45°; they were also wider and longer than replacement brick chambers. The replacement of the turf-sided Monkey Marsh Lock, as elsewhere, does not mean the obliteration of the original chamber; this will remain for posterity as an example of these unique structures.

The eastern outskirts of Newbury throw up sporadic industry, the crossing of the railway being an unintentional boundary between town and country. 'Twixt Reading and Bristol, there are few 'straights' of any note … perhaps it is this, the 'unexpected' just around the corner, that draws so many to Britain's watery arteries. On the other hand for the working boatman meanders meant time and money, so the so-called Long Cut south of Thatcham must have been a welcome, if brief, experience. Save for the woods between Widmead Lock (89) and the wanderings of the Kennet, the terrain is generally open with pastures to the south and Thatcham Marsh to the north. The latter was once a mix of water-meadows and osier beds but is today an important ecological site, a safe retreat for the reed and sedge warbler and other rare species.

> "After we had passed the lock our engine pulled up dead, and we found so much refuse, ropes, rags, wires and even a button-stick wound round the propeller, that it could not be cleared even after several hours' work …"

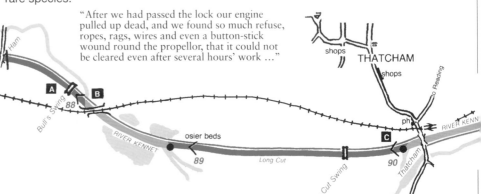

THATCHAM
In recent years, as though to re-establish its superiority over neighbouring Newbury, Thatcham has been expanding in all directions – though not as yet across the A4. The hub of its shopping facilities lies about a mile north of the navigation.
Sustenance
SWAN HOTEL – large hostelry with restaurant; just north of Thatcham Bridge. Other pubs include: WHITE HART, CRICKETS, KING'S HEAD, WHEATSHEAF (on the A4) and OLD CHEQUERS.
SZECHUAN INN – good value Peking cuisine; in the town, close to the A4. Other snack bars, etc; also HUSSAIN'S INDIAN CUISINE restaurant and take-away.
Shops
All major banks and basics.
Public Transport
RAIL – good connections on the Newbury-Reading-London line; details on 0345 484950.
ROAD – good Newbury Buses services to and from Newbury/Reading; details from Newbury (01635) 40743.

Restoration
Bull's Lock (88) was the victim of vandalism in 1954 and remained out of commission until rebuilt by K&ACT volunteer labour in 1976. Turf-sided Widmead and Monkey Marsh Locks (89 & 90) fell into disrepair in the early 50s when navigation ceased west of Heale's (93) and east of Greenham Swing Bridge (now 'up-and-over'). Restoration of both was completed in 1990.

FOR THE BOATER
Boaters should be aware of the influence of the river Kennet's current, especially where it leaves or joins a man-made section of the navigation.

> Never leave a WINDLASS on a PADDLE SPINDLE

Some swing bridges can only be unlocked with a windlass.

> Always SLOW DOWN when passing MOORED CRAFT

> If you are making a WASH you are going TOO FAST

All crafts using the river Kennet should carry an anchor.

Although the chimney of Colthrop Paper Mill used to dominate the skyline here, its attendant industrial estate remains an unexpected intrusion on the largely open terrain. To the south the wandering Kennet keeps itself to itself while the man-made alternative takes a more direct, albeit windswept, course … though there is some respite from the risk of windburn in the lee of the woods near Woolhampton. It is strange to think that none of this might exist had a scheme to solve London's water needs, mooted in 1892, come to fruition. The idea was to construct a huge reservoir in the Kennet valley by forming a lake from about a mile east of Newbury to Aldermaston, submerging the villages of Woolhampton and Aldermaston, several mills and parts of the A4, the railway and the canal. Perhaps the chimney at Colthrop would have been the only surviving landmark!

Restoration
Colthrop and Midgham Locks (91 & 92) were victims of the general neglect of the early 50s. Heale's (93), on the other hand, was the main cause of the 'turf-sided' problems back in 1950; it was rebuilt in 1952 but didn't last and, like its neighbour, Woolhampton (94), soon fell foul of lack of maintenance; it was restored in 1987. Restoration of Heale's and Midgham was complete by 1989 and through navigation re-established the following year.

A Colthrop Mill: Colthrop Board & Paper Mill complex is not one of the most aesthetic of canalside industries. But then such was the *raison d'être* of the canal. A working canal was not all green-ness and light. It was a vibrant working artery that, through the march of 'progress', has largely reverted to its 'natural' beginnings. There has been a paper mill on this site since 1805 … *its* remains, were they here, might possibly be a little more pleasing to the eye!

B Roman Road: At the east of the Colthrop site the navigation severs what was the Roman road from Speen to Silchester. Five such roads converge south-west of Reading at Silchester (Calleva Atrebatum); one of these heads north-west to Cirencester, branching off around Speen to Bath. The road is thus one of Britain's earliest east-west arteries; hundreds of years later the Kennet & Avon was blazing the same trail only to find that it too was dispensable.

C Broad and Narrow: Here on the Kennet Navigation, there are, for historical reasons, locks of varying lengths and widths though basically they are all termed 'broad'. Britain's inland canal and river navigations largely fall into two types – broad and narrow; the former normally having locks around 14ft wide and 70ft long, the latter being the same length but half the width. The K&A's origins determined its broadness, in that both the Kennet & Avon Navigations were built to accommodate river and/or estuarial craft which were normally wide-beamed – there would have been little point in constructing a 'narrow' link. As trade on the K&A declined, the narrowboat started to replace the barge, hitherto the mainstay of the carrying trade; as loads became 'lighter' they could easily cope and, of course, they were faster. In the 1830s, one Bath carrier advertised that his new 'fly' service was using narrow boats "in lieu of heavy Barges"; it is known that such horse-drawn craft could reach speeds exceeding 10mph.

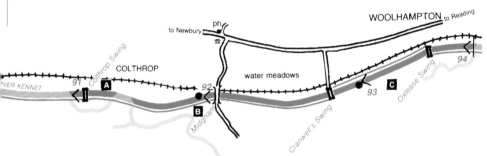

MIDGHAM
The village itself lies amid the wooded hillside to the north of the A4, its leafy lanes and olde worlde cottages, like the navigation, light years away from the modern-day hubbub of the Bath Road.

Sustenance
COACH AND HORSES – bar food in attractive roadside inn; on the A4, ⅓ mile north of Midgham Bridge.
Public Transport
ROAD – regular Newbury Buses services on A4; details from Newbury (01635) 40743.

NEWBURY

An ancient ballad reveals that King John, fleeing from the wrath of his barons, hid in Newbury at the house of an "old spinning woman". Whether or not it was because of the yarn he spun her, medieval Newbury gradually grew to prominence as a cloth-making centre, its most famous clothier being John Winchcombe, better known as Jack o'Newbury. By the 17th century trade had already begun to decline and, despite Sir John Throckmorton's efforts (see opposite) to rekindle some of the pride lost to the northern mills, the inevitable happened, with the result that few of the area's mills survived.

Rivalries of a different kind put Newbury on the map during the Civil War when two major battles were fought in the area; the first was in 1643 at Wash Common and the second the following year close to Donnington Castle. The final score was a 2:0 win to the Parliamentarians though the Royalists eventually won the replay at Donnington.

A 19th-century gazetteer described the town thus: "Newbury consists of broad and well-paved streets and presents a solid and quiet appearance … A neat stone bridge takes the principal thorough-fare across the Kennet." Should his ghost ever pass this way again, it would find the bridge with little difficulty … but where would it park on a Saturday?

Shopping
Newbury is a medium-sized town and thus caters for most shopping needs with the Market Place used as originally intended on Thursdays and Saturdays. The town is particularly proud of its purpose-built pedestrian area, the Kennet Centre.

Sustenance
The town boasts a fairly wide selection of watering holes and eating places, including several take-aways and the almost obligatory pizza-parlour. This is Courage country but other breweries have an impressive representation.

Pubs
HATCHET – large inviting inn with enticing range of food; in the market place.
HOBGOBLIN – un-tarted up, traditional pub serving a range of bar food ('Hobgobbles'); at the town end of Bartholomew Street.
RAT & PARROT – good bar food behind an attractive brick frontage; in Bartholomew Street.
TAP & SPILE – bar snacks available in a 'local' atmosphere amid the hustle and bustle of the main shopping street.
UNCLE HENRY'S – good pub food in a friendly atmosphere tucked away down Marsh Lane just off Northbrook Street.

Eating Out
VALLE D'ORO – Excellent Italian food served up and cooked by two enterprising Spaniards; at the junction of Oxford Street and Bath Road.
BRUNO'S – good value basic meals and snacks tucked away at the end of an alley-way off Oxford Street.
CURRY GARDEN – well-presented Tandoori House in London Road, close to the Clock Tower.
MADAGASCAN GIN PALACE – restaurant with an exotic menu, including various oriental and caribbean dishes; in picturesque Inch's Yard, just off Market Street.

Entertainments
WATERMILL THEATRE – based two miles to the north-west at Bagnor alongside a mill-stream on the river Lambourn; tel: Newbury (01635) 46044.

Exhibitions/Museums
WEST BERKSHIRE MUSEUM – The Wharf; tel: Newbury (01635) 30511. The Museum's two adjoining buildings, the Cloth Hall and the old wharfside Granary, are themselves illustrative of Newbury's past.

Sightseeing
ST NICHOLAS CHURCH – this large church by West Mills was built during the 16th century, at the height of the town's prosperity; it boasts an unusual 17th-century pulpit.
DONNINGTON CASTLE – the ruined, tall, towered gatehouse is all that remains of the castle that featured in one of the Civil War's most memorable sieges; a mile to the north-west between the A4 and A34.
WASH COMMON – the site of an earlier Civil War (1643) blood-bath is about a mile to the south-west of the town.

Racing
For details of local racing fixtures tel: Newbury (01635) 40015.

Information
TOURIST INFORMATION CENTRE – West Berkshire Museum, The Wharf, Newbury RG14 5AS; tel: Newbury (01635) 30267.

Public Transport
RAIL – Newbury, Station Approach; for details of services tel: 0345 484950.
ROAD – Bus Station, Market Street; tel: Newbury (01635) 40743.

ILLUSTRATIVE OF
MANUFACTURING CELERITY
TO PROVE THE POSSIBILITY OF
WOOL
BEING MANUFACTURED INTO
CLOTH
AND MADE INTO A
COAT
BETWEEN
SUNRISE AND SUNSET
AND WHICH WAS SUCCESSFULLY ACCOMPLISHED ON
TUESDAY, the 25th of JUNE, 1811.
AT FIVE O'CLOCK THAT MORNING
TWO SHEEP
BELONGING TO
Sir John Throckmorton, Bart.
WERE SHEARED BY HIS OWN SHEPHERD—
FRANCIS DRUETT
AND THE WOOL GIVEN TO
Mr. JOHN COXETER
AT GREENHAM MILLS, NEAR
NEWBURY, BERKSHIRE:
WHO HAD
The WOOL Spun, The YARN Spooled, Warped, Loomed, and Wove. The CLOTH Burred, Milled, Rowed, Dyed, Dried, Sheared, and Pressed
BY FOUR O'CLOCK - ALL the processes of MANUFACTURE were performed BY HAND in ELEVEN HOURS.
THE CLOTH was then given to
Mr. ISAAC WHITE, Tailor, of Newbury, Whose Son, James White, cut the Coat out and had it made up within
TWO HOURS AND TWENTY MINUTES,
When the Master Manufacturer, Mr. John Coxeter, presented it to
Sir John Throckmorton, Bart.
who appeared with it on before an assembly of 5000 spectators who had come far and near to witness this singular and unprecedented performance completed in
THIRTEEN HOURS AND TWENTY MINUTES.

READING

Many will think of Reading as a Thames-side town but its roots are firmly astride that lesser flow, the river Kennet. The great Kennetside Benedictine Abbey (consecrated by Thomas à Becket), which dominated the town for 400 years, fell foul of the Reformation and, stripped of its wealth, soon became no more than a ruin … aided and abetted by the recycling instincts of the townsfolk. What little they left – mainly the magnificent gateway – remains as a monument to Reading's medieval stature.

Within the shadow of the Abbey ruins the cloth industry developed and flourished along the Kennet and soon became the mainstay of the Reading economy. But fate intervened in the shape of the Civil War and the town not only suffered heavily through the 'natural' process of changing hands several times but also through the inevitable depletion of its hitherto economic base.

Fortune was on Reading's side, though it did not show its hand until the early 18th century when the Kennet Navigation opened up trade routes between London and Newbury with Reading the natural benefactor. With almost indecent haste further east-west routes were opened or extended – the canal, the coach roads and the railway – and the town began to flourish once more.

Bulbs, beer and biscuits brought identity and prosperity, just as Oscar Wilde brought notoriety through his *Ballad of Reading Gaol*, where he was an inmate for two years.

Reading has clung to its past and is using it to shape its future; like Bristol it has experimented with concrete but has settled for the warmth of brick. Kennetside Reading in particular is slowly evolving as a winner in the battle between environmental architecture and expedience.

Shopping

Two thoroughfares, Broad Street and Friar Street cater for almost every shopping need; in addition there's the under-cover compactness of three malls – Broad Street, Friar's Walk and (from Autumn 1999) the Oracle, between Bridge Street and Minster Street, which will also house Warner Brothers Cinemas and the Jelly Leg'd Chicken Arts Riverside Gallery. A general market operates Wednesday to Saturday in Hosier Street. Reading has been dubbed a 'typical' British town; it is thus not uncommon to find new products being 'tested' locally.

Sustenance

As almost every taste is catered for, the following can only be a basic guide to what is available … there is no substitute for wandering round the streets eyeing up all the menus or trying to find a pub that isn't a Courage house!

Pubs

YE BOAR'S HEAD – good selection of hot and cold lunchtime fare; in Friar Street.
TUDOR TAVERN – fine Elizabethan, panelled room in Friar Street hostelry, though no longer serving food.
RAT & PARROT – Market Place pub with a range of bar meals.
HORN – hot and cold bar food in impressive inn; next to the Broad Street Mall.

Eating Out

CHRONICLES – quietly situated just behind the Town Hall, with full food menu; in Valpy Street.
WINE CELLAR – Wine merchant with attractive, corner café, serving snacks and house wines; in Oxford Road.
HA! HA! – spacious, up-market, stylish watering hole; riverside in King's Road.
NINO'S – cheerful, family-run, Italian restaurant in Market Place.
PEPE SALE – Sardinian cuisine in large restaurant in Queen's Walk, behind the Broad Street Mall.
PAD THAI – large restaurant with extensive Thai menu; on the corner of Hosier Street and Queen's Walk.
GEORGE HOTEL – an erstwhile coaching inn with several levels of eating; on the corner of King's Road and Minster Street.

Entertainments

THE HEXAGON – a multi-purpose entertainments centre behind the Butts Centre; tel: Reading (0118) 960 6060.
ODEON CINEMAS – Cheapside; tel: Reading (0118) 957 6803.

Exhibitions/Museums

MUSEUM OF READING – Blagrave Street; tel: Reading (0118) 939 9800.
MUSEUM OF ENGLISH RURAL LIFE – The University, Whiteknights; tel: Reading (0118) 931 8660.
URE MUSEUM OF GREEK ARCHAEOLOGY – The University, Whiteknights; tel: Reading (0118) 931 8420.
COLE MUSEUM OF ZOOLOGY – specimens from all over the world; The University, Whiteknights; tel: Reading (0118) 931 8903.
BLAKE'S LOCK MUSEUM – waterways and industrial heritage exhibitions; weekend afternoons only, plus Tuesday-Friday in school holidays; Kennetside, off Gasworks Road; tel: Reading (0118) 939 0918.

Sightseeing

ABBEY GATEWAY AND RUINS – founded in 1121, it saw much medieval pageantry before falling into a state of decay; linked to the river loop by Chestnut Walk.
FORBURY GARDENS – unexpected peace and quiet under the gaze of the massive Maiwand Lion; close to the Abbey ruins.
ST MARY'S CHURCH – a site of worship for over 1,000 years, the current building's chequer-board tower and flint walls (parts of the re-cycled Abbey) date from 1550; opposite the Broad Street Mall.
RIVER THAMES – Reading's other river is worth a visit; a walk north-west from Kennet Mouth takes in Caversham Lock and some pleasant stretches before returning via Caversham Bridge. Regular boat trips to Mapledurham (0118 948 1088) and Henley (0118 957 2388) leave here during the 'season'.

Information

TOURIST INFORMATION CENTRE – The Town Hall, Blagrave Street, Reading RG1 1QH; tel: Reading (0118) 956 6226.

Public Transport

RAIL – Reading, Station Hill; details on 0345 484950.
ROAD – Railway Station, Station Hill; tel: Reading (0118) 959 4000.

A Woolhampton Swing Bridge: When a lock deteriorates its demise is generally obvious – boaters and walkers alike share in its indignity. Swing bridges are more subtle; their condition is altogether less conspicuous … and far from moving. In 1940, Tom and Angela Rolt encountered such an 'invalid' here: "With half the able-bodied males of the village heaving on crow-bars under the direction of the red-faced landlord of the 'Row Barge' and with Cressy going full astern, her bow line fast to a bridge railing post, it took us three hours to open the bridge at Woolhampton".

B Midgham Station: Midgham Station serves the Woolhampton area, the name Woolhampton having been dropped back in GWR days when it was apt to be confused with Wolverhampton!

C Aldermaston Mill: The Kennet remains technically navigable for a further ⅓ mile south of its junction with the Salmon Cut as far as Aldermaston Mill. Corn was once carried by barge direct to the mill which stands at the confluence of the rivers Enborne and Kennet. Today the mill, minus its top two storeys, is available for private functions.

D Aldermaston Wharf: Situated just to the east of the new lift bridge, Aldermaston Wharf played a major role in the early Kennet Navigation. Local timber and related products, malt and flour all found outlets to greater markets via the wharf. In 1852, when the GWR had taken over control of the K&A, a second wharf was created as an interchange point between canal and railway at the end of a short spur north of the lock.

E Aldermaston Lift Bridge: For many years the 'fixed' swing bridge at Aldermaston was seen as a major obstruction to restoration at the eastern end of the navigation. Ironically the problem was solved by a hi-tech hydraulic replacement which remained 'cut-off' for several years by seemingly less major restoration works.

F Padworth Lower Wharf: Unusually, this small wharf is on the towpath side of the navigation; it is now British Waterways' depot for the eastern section.

Here is one of the most delightful river sections. The Kennet dons its coat of green east of Woolhampton, its secluded valley twisting and turning along its narrow time-worn course. The artificial cut, part of which is known as Salmon Cut, couldn't be more different, its more direct route having a remoter feel, despite the proximity of the railway and the A4. Osier (a species of willow, tough, pliant branches of which are used in basket work) beds were once a feature of the landscape where road, rail and canal converge near Padworth. While extolling on nature's whims it is easy to forget that man's contribution, even 20th-century man's, to the landscape is by no means always negative. Aldermaston Lock (95) is a case in point for the unusual scalloped brickwork of its restoration is nothing short of magnificent. Aldermaston itself lies off the canal and features in the walk on page 64.

"Another great difficulty that we encountered was that of getting under the numerous foot-bridges, cow-bridges and traffic-bridges which often could not be opened after years of disuse, and that did not provide the necessary head-room that we required."

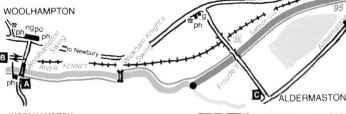

Restoration
This section, along with Heale's and Woolhampton Locks (93 & 94) to the west and six locks to the east, were part of the 8-mile stoppage which took effect in May 1950. Dereliction was inevitable and Aldermaston (95), Padworth (96) and Towney (97) needed re-building; the latter was re-opened in 1976, the two former along with Padworth Swing Bridge were re-opened in late 1987.

WOOLHAMPTON
A main road village with its roots in the mail coach services along the old Bath Road.
Sustenance
ROWBARGE INN – welcoming inn with good food and occasional live music; canalside by Woolhampton Swing Bridge.
ANGEL INN – restaurant and B&B in roadside hostelry; ¼ mile north of Woolhampton Swing Bridge.
FALMOUTH ARMS – large roadside inn with bar snacks; ¼ mile north of Woolhampton Swing Bridge.

ALDERMASTON WHARF
A canalside settlement that has its origins in the old Kennet Navigation.
Sustenance
BUTT INN – restaurant and bar snacks – a friendly place with an amazing collection of key-rings; also B&B; 200 yards south of Aldermaston Lift Bridge.
HARE & HOUNDS – bar snacks and grills in road-side inn; ½ mile north-west of Padworth Bridge.
K&A TRUST VISITORS' CENTRE – small range of snacks and ices; canalside.

THE ROWBARGE

Sightseeing
ALDERMASTON MILL and ALDERMASTON VILLAGE feature in the circular walk described on page 64.
Public Transport
RAIL – services to and from Woolhampton (Midgham Station) and Aldermaston on the Reading-Newbury line; details on 0345 484950.
ROAD – regular Newbury Buses services along A4 between Newbury and Reading; details from Newbury (01635) 40743.

FOR THE BOATER
A BW key is required to operate Aldermaston Lift Bridge; boaters should keep strictly to the instructions that explain when and how the bridge can be operated.

Boaters should be aware of the influence of the river Kennet's current, especially where it leaves or joins a man-made section of the navigation.

Some swing bridges can only be unlocked with a windlass.

Frouds Bridge Marina, Frouds Lane, Aldermaston RG7 4LH; tel: Reading (0118) 971 4508; Water, gas, diesel, 'Elsan' disposal, pump-out, rubbish disposal, chandlery, boat sales, moorings, K&A windlasses, BW keys and licences.

Reading Marine Company, Aldermaston Wharf, Padworth RG7 4JS; tel: Reading (0118) 971 3666; 2-12 berth hire-craft, water, gas, diesel, rubbish disposal, pump-out, boat & engine repairs, cranage, safety inspections, moorings, chandlery, K&A windlasses and BW keys.

East-bound travellers will have become increasingly aware of the natural river sections while west-bound the river seems to be becoming less of an influence. There is no contradiction for between Ufton and Theale the 'blend' is at its most regular with alternate snatches of river and man-made cuts and locks. Cuts or not, the feel of river dominates for this is truly the valley of the Kennet, its sinuous meanders never far from the navigation. Two of the cuts avoid old mill buildings, Tyle and Shenfield Mills, while by way of compensation, the tree-lined Sulhamstead Cut offers a sylvan, albeit remote, alternative to the generally open aspect. Nowhere is this more apparent than around the old water-filled gravel workings, most of which have been landscaped and reclaimed for leisure use.

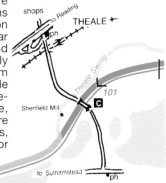

Restoration
The shallow Ufton Lock (98) was a late addition to the navigation and was dispensed with when Towney was rebuilt in 1976. Tyle Mill (99) was repaired in 1973 but remained out of commission until 1976 due to swing-bridge problems. By 1953, Sulhamstead (100) was the limit of navigation west from the Thames – it was re-opened in 1968. Sheffield (101) was operable as a turf-sided lock into the 70s but rebuilt in 1980.

A Ufton Cut and Lock: Until the 1830s the short loop of river south of Ufton New Cut was a part of the navigable Kennet. At that time a new cut was constructed which included a shallow lock (its rise/fall was a mere 1ft 9in) to improve the head of water up-cut and below Towney Lock (97). Although Ufton Cut remains, Ufton Lock has been degated, it being redundant – in terms of its original function – now that Towney's old turf-sided chamber has been replaced by a new one a little further upstream.

B Sulhamstead Lock: With the navigation rapidly falling into a state of disrepair, aided and abetted by disinterest and disregard during the late 1940s and early 50s, it is not surprising that by 1953 Sulhamstead Lock (100) was the limit of navigation from the Thames. For a time (1955-59) this was reduced by a further 2½ Miles to Burghfield Lock (103) but it was not until 1965, when Burghfield again caused problems, that work began on rebuilding Sulhamstead. The restoration of Sulhamstead is especially important in that it inaugurated the concept of 'co-operation' between the Kennet & Avon Canal Trust and British Waterways – the former would raise the money with which the latter would initiate restoration. The original lock was one of those built to accommodate the wide 'Newbury' barges (see below) and so it was possible to construct a new chamber within the old – ironically, it is now the navigation's smallest lock. The work was carried out by, among others, prisoners from Oxford Gaol, plant being provided by the Royal Engineers.

C Shenfield Lock and 'Newbury' Barges: A lock with two names, Shenfield and/or Sheffield – though there seems less doubt that the nearby mill was called Shenfield. This was originally a turf-sided lock but was, like Aldermaston, restored by building on the scalloped brickwork below water level. Such brickwork was an innovation of the 1760s when locks were enlarged to accommodate the 109ft x 17ft 'Newbury' barges which besides being large, carried a crew of six men and a boy, and could require as many as 14 horses to pull them upstream. By 1830 only a few were still trading so a further rebuilding of some locks to smaller dimensions was not a disaster … unless, that is, you owned a 'Newbury' barge.

FOR THE BOATER
Boaters should be aware of the influence of the river Kennet's current, especially where it leaves or joins a man-made section of the navigation.

Boaters should never leave the mainstream of the navigation.

> Never leave a WINDLASS on a PADDLE SPINDLE

Some swing bridges can only be unlocked with a windlass.

On fast-flowing river sections, upstream traffic should give way to downstream, especially at bridges.

All craft using the Kennet should carry an anchor.

UFTON GREEN
A peaceful hamlet, complete with ivy-clad church ruin, built round a small triangular green, south-east of the navigation.
Sustenance
WINNING HAND – restaurant and B&B; on A4 ½ mile north of Ufton Swing Bridge.

SULHAMSTEAD
A scattered parish south-east of the Kennet which includes Sulhamstead Abbots and Sulhamstead Bannister; the former boasts a small flint-built church with a timber bell-turret dating from 1200.
Sustenance
MULLIGANS – fish restaurant and oyster bar; on A4 ½ mile north-west of Tyle Mill Swing Bridge.

THEALE
The M4 and its attendant by-pass have saved Theale from the worst ravages of Motoring Man. Though Roman and Saxon remains have been found, its more recent past and many of its buildings have stage-coaching connections.
Sustenance
RAILWAY ARMS – bar snacks; ½ mile north of Theale Swing Bridge.
FOX & HOUNDS – restaurant and bar food; ½ mile south of Theale Swing Bridge. Other Theale pubs include: RED LION, CROWN, LAMB, BULL, VOLUNTEER and FALCON.
Shops
All the basics plus Lloyds cashpoint.
Sightseeing
THEALE PARISH CHURCH – the massive 19th-century church seems somehow out of place. It was a present to the parish from one Sophie Shepperd whose tomb lies within the chantry chapel.
Public Transport
RAIL – regular services between Reading and Newbury; details on 0345 484950.
ROAD – local Newbury Buses services; details from Newbury (01635) 40743.

A Garston Turf-sided Lock: Garston Lock (102) remains as the sole working example of a turf-sided lock (see page 42) on the Kennet & Avon. The fate of such locks is bound up with our modern concept of safety and what some see as the inherent dangers in the lack of an upper retaining wall. It remains to be seen whether Garston will eventually succumb to these pressures or remain as a rare example of 'living' history. Isolated locks such as Garston were easily transformed – especially during the GWR-enforced closure between Saturday and Sunday – into makeshift dry-docks, the boat being supported on timbers spanning the lower chamber walls.

B Burghfield Cut and Lock: During the 1830s a new channel was cut westwards from just above Burghfield Lock (103) and, as at Ufton (see page 47), the new Burghfield Cut by-passed the circuitous wanderings of the Kennet. The replacement Burghfield Lock and its neighbour at Sulhamstead (100), are the canal's shortest.

C Southcote Pumping Station: The Victorian brick building that oversees Southcote Lock (104) is the redundant Southcote Pumping Station which, when opened in 1850, was the key to Reading's demanding water needs.

D Cruiseway and Remainder Status: Under the 1968 Transport Act, Britain's BW-administered waterways were divided into three categories: commercial, 'cruiseway' and 'remainder'. The last two were applied to the K&A in that the navigation had three 'cruiseway' and two 'remainder' sections, their difference in status being the level to which BW was required to maintain them. From the tail of Tyle Mill Lock (99) to High Bridge, Reading (which includes this stretch), from the tail of Hamstead Lock (81) to the head of Bull's Lock (88), to the Avon, between Hanham Lock (1) and Bath, were all designated 'cruiseway' and BW was obliged to maintain these to navigable standards. What was left was 'the remainder', a phrase which stuck and applied to those sections of the K&A (and other waterways) which BW only had to maintain to a standard compatible with the interest of public health and safety. Things have moved on since then and within the life of this guide all its waters should have gained 'cruiseway' status.

West-bound travellers might be excused for momentarily relishing the strong stone curves of Burghfield Bridge for it is the last such structure before Newbury. The more modern crossing of the M4 scarcely bears comparison – its cold-grey span extending into the green yonder, its monotonous drone reverberating across the countryside. But such man-made monstrosities, however necessary, cannot compete with the natural time-worn course of the Kennet, its verdant valley scarcely touched by the nearby conurbation. Between erstwhile gravel pits and osier beds, the navigation asserts its authority on the landscape, revelling in its not infrequent flirtations with tree-lined tunnels and gently rolling farmland. It is not only in Berkeley Square that you can enjoy the song of the nightingale for the damp willow scrub hereabouts is home territory to several pairs.

Restoration
Garston (102) remains as the only fully working example of a turf-sided lock – there are no plans for its replacement. Burghfield (turf-sided) Lock (103) was deemed unsafe back in 1950 and was closed for nine years; by 1965 it was in such poor state that rebuilding was necessary (1968). Though in need of extensive repairs in the 50s, Southcote and Fobney Locks (104 & 105) have not required rebuilding.

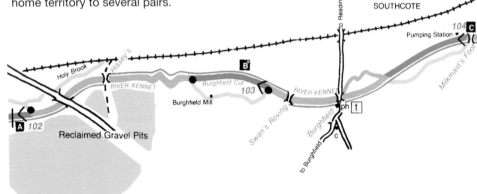

BURGHFIELD BRIDGE
The small village of Burghfield lies two miles to the south.
Sustenance
CUNNING MAN – wide selection of hot and cold food; waterside by Burghfield Bridge.
BRIDGE CAFE – welcoming snacks almost in the middle of nowhere; 200 yds south of Burghfield Bridge.

FOR THE BOATER
Care should be taken at the series of sharp – and blind — bends between Burghfield Cut and the M4; where two craft meet, upstream traffic should give way if necessary to boats travelling downstream.

Always SLOW DOWN when passing MOORED CRAFT

Some swing bridges can only be unlocked with a windlass.

Boaters should be aware of the influence of the river Kennet's current, especially where it leaves or joins a man-made section of the navigation.

Boaters should never leave the mainstream of the navigation.

All craft using the Kennet should carry an anchor.

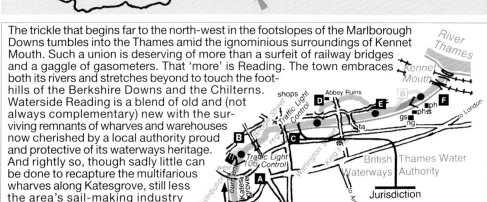

The trickle that begins far to the north-west in the footslopes of the Marlborough Downs tumbles into the Thames amid the ignominious surroundings of Kennet Mouth. Such a union is deserving of more than a surfeit of railway bridges and a gaggle of gasometers. That 'more' is Reading. The town embraces both its rivers and stretches beyond to touch the foothills of the Berkshire Downs and the Chilterns. Waterside Reading is a blend of old and (not always complementary) new with the surviving remnants of wharves and warehouses now cherished by a local authority proud and protective of its waterways heritage. And rightly so, though sadly little can be done to recapture the multifarious wharves along Katesgrove, still less the area's sail-making industry which, it is said, contributed much to Nelson's victory at Trafalgar.

"In many places the locks were in a hopeless and even dangerous condition, and several times we were ordered out of the boat in case the gates collapsed under the pressure of the water."

For the Walker
At present there is no riverside path between High Bridge and the Inner Distribution Road Bridge though this is gradually being rectified. There are two alternative routes, the longer to the north, the shorter to the south. Both are marked on the map though the northern alternative is the more interesting except, that is, for those who have a penchant for bus garages and busy inner-city traffic.

FOR THE BOATER
The section between County Lock (106) and High Bridge is controlled by traffic lights and includes a particularly narrow stretch known as Brewery Gut. Boaters should heed all instructions at both ends and only proceed when the green light shows. Under no circumstances should boats tie up between the traffic lights. Brewery Gut is fast-flowing even when other parts of the navigation appear relatively sedate; boaters should allow for this flow when manoeuvering, etc.

All craft using the Kennet should carry an anchor.

Craft navigating the K&A will require a special windlass.

Kennet Cruises, 14 Beech Lane, Earley, Reading RG6 5PT; tel: Reading (0118) 987 1115 or (0831) 326482. 4 berth hire-craft.

Berrybrook Boats, 195 Henley Road, Caversham, Reading RG4 6LJ; tel: (0831) 574673; hire-craft.

Bridge Boats, Fry's Island, De Montford Road, Reading RG1 8DG; tel: Reading (0118) 959 0346; 2-12 berth hire-craft.

READING
Information on Reading is detailed on page 45; riverside facilities only are detailed below.
Sustenance
KENNET ARMS – bar snacks and live music; by Berkeley Avenue Bridge.
WARWICK ARMS – bar snacks; on King's Road between the river loop and the mainstream.
WYNFORD ARMS – bar meals; on King's Road between the river loop and the mainstream.
FISHERMAN'S COTTAGE – excellent hot and cold menu and occasional live music; riverside west of Blake's Lock.
JOLLY ANGLER – hot and cold meals and snacks; riverside east of Blake's Lock.

A County Lock: County Lock (106) is officially the last lock on the navigation though there is one other between here and Kennet Mouth (see below). The lock was originally sited on the other side of the river by what was Bear Wharf, the infilling of the latter and the re-siting of the former both having taken place in the mid-1870s. Some interesting buildings remain, mostly connected with the brewing interests of William Simmonds.

B Brewery Gut: In the 1880s Simmonds Brewery bought the towpath alongside the winding river section between Bridge Street and High Bridge, built on it and forced the river into a narrower and deeper channel. Almost at a stroke was the infamous Brewery Gut conceived. Today its circuitous and occasionally cavernous course is regulated by traffic lights … the working boatman had no such help and, engineless, found ingenious ways (not dissimilar to those used at Newbury's Town Bridge – see page 41) of circumventing the horse.

C High Bridge and Wharf: Before the new stone 'high' bridge was built across the Kennet in 1787, this was, for many craft trading off the Thames, the limit of navigation. Not surprisingly, several wharves sprang up downstream of the bridge, the area around the most westerly, High Bridge Wharf, becoming the trading centre of a bustling market town. The through-route to Bristol brought prosperity and expansion and, despite the eventual decline in trade, the wharf remained open until the mid-1940s.

D Medieval Quay: Recent excavations of the 'Abbey' loop of the river have revealed the timber piling remains of what was clearly a medieval wharf.

E Huntley & Palmers: Biscuits travel best by water … it is thus not surprising that in 1849 Messrs Huntley & Palmers moved to Reading to exploit the trading possibilities of the Kennet. All water-borne trade – flour in, biscuits out – ceased during the war, and the factory has been subsumed into the new Oracle Centre.

F Blake's Lock: This is the gateway to and from the Thames. Originally a flash lock, Blake's is the only lock not on the Thames maintained by the Thames Conservancy. Today it is overseen by tasteful riverside housing that complements the setting.

Navigating from Sharpness to Bristol

The Kennet & Avon can never be part of a 'loop' or 'ring' for, to all intents and purposes, the 'missing link' will always be the Sharpness-Bristol section which is definitely not recommended for inland craft. Nevertheless, during the early 80s, as restoration of the Kennet & Avon progressed and more and more of the canal re-opened east from Bath, owners of inland craft were increasingly tempted to take on this potentially hazardous journey from the Gloucester & Sharpness Canal, the nearest connection with the main body of Britain's inland waterways network. Though these pages may make it all look easy, they are, by definition, aimed at the experienced boater, the boater who not only has confidence in his or her boat but is also not going to be intimidated by all that water. By far the simplest way to make the trip is to join a convoy of escorted boats already committed to it, the most obvious being the flotilla of craft that annually (in August) come down the estuary to take part in the Bristol Regatta. Being a weekend event, there is little scope for boaters to explore the Avon to Bath or beyond so the return trip may still have to be unaccompanied though there is the alternative of the 'long way round'. Whether you opt for the convoy or decide to go it alone, the following information should be supplemented by Bristol Harbour's *Information for Boat Owners*, an invaluable, detailed and uncomplicated guide to both the seaward approaches to Bristol and the Floating Harbour.

At Sharpness

Make contact with BW's Dock Office and make sure they know of your intended passage. Should you require pilotage – a must if you cannot read a navigation chart – they will arrange this … at a price; here too you can get information on tides and related locking times out of Sharpness Lock. Also telephone Bristol's Dockmaster and be prepared to tell him – or his answering machine – the following: name and telephone number; description, name and length of craft; whether or not you will use VHF on your approach to Bristol; date and estimated time of departure from Sharpness and arrival at Bristol. As the journey involves 'sitting out' a tide at the mouth of the Avon, try to choose a day that has *two* daylight tides; this is, of course, only likely during the summer months. Finally, before setting off, check the forecast weather conditions by contacting Marinecall Weather (see page 51) for a local two-day inshore forecast.

Between Sharpness and Avonmouth

Though boaters have made this trip armed with only an OS map, Admiralty Chart 1166 is advised. This clearly plots the route through and round the many sandbanks and rocks and under the imposing spans of the two Severn Bridges, the M48 and M4. On the approach to Avonmouth the tide will be well and truly on the ebb and passage up the Avon cannot be undertaken until the next tide.

At Avonmouth

There are several ways of 'sitting out' the tide at Avonmouth. The safest is to pay your dues and lock into Avonmouth's Royal Edward Dock (1) but this is only possible if you can catch the last locking of the ebbing tide – not always feasible in the time it takes to get down the estuary from Sharpness. The other alternatives are to drop anchor across the estuary in the lee of the pier at Portishead (2), or to sit it out on the mud a little way up the Avon by the old lock entrance (3); in an emergency the pier across the estuary at Portway Dock will offer protection (4). The first locking into Bristol is 2hrs 35mins before high water so set off up-river from Avonmouth with the tide about 3$^{1}/_{2}$-4hrs before high water. Should you miss this locking there are two more before the tide turns – see table opposite.

On the Avon

The Avon is relatively simple to navigate; Admiralty Chart 1859, though useful, is not essential. Pilotage is available up 'the ditch', as the estuary pilots affectionately know it, but, if you've made it thus far it's scarcely worth the expense. Keep midstream, look out for the sand dredgers and enjoy the scenery which, after the exhilarating vastness of the estuary, has an altogether more friendly feel.

The village of Pill on the south bank was once known as the 'pilot's village', an appellation dating back to the 19th century when cutters based here, sailed down the Bristol Channel seeking out ships to guide into Bristol. As a side-line, the inhabitants of Pill and neighbouring hamlets were not averse to indulging in a little smuggling. Above Pill is Horseshoe Bend which straightens into the rocky wooded chasm of the Avon Gorge, a favoured challenge to rock climbers from near and far. Almost without warning the gorge is dominated by the magnificent span of Clifton Suspension Bridge, Brunel's spectacular masterpiece that has been dubbed the 'Gateway to Bristol'.

Gloucester & Sharpness Canal

SHARPNESS

Lydney

Chepstow

M48

M4

Severn Estuary

AVONMOUTH

1

3

4

2

M5

Pill

PORTISHEAD

BRISTOL FLOATING HARBOUR

Docking Signals

Entrance Lock

Gridiron Dock Office

Junction Lock *(not normally in use)*

New Cut

Harbour Master's Office

BRISTOL

At Bristol

The way in to the Entrance Lock to Cumberland Basin is on the left just round the bend from Clifton Suspension Bridge. On the bend itself, look out for the Docking Signals and don't proceed towards the lock until green shows (red obviously means 'wait'). Boats equipped with VHF will already have been in contact with the Dockmaster as per the instructions in the *Information for Boat Owners*. Assuming your arrival has been anticipated, and having locked through into Cumberland Basin, you should tie up at the south-west corner of the Basin and go ashore to seek out and pay any dues to the Dockmaster (assuming these have not been pre-paid). If you arrive too late to lock in, then you will have to sit out another tide; the best place to do this is atop the Gridiron – see map.

It is worth repeating that this trip, though not over-complicated, is not to be undertaken lightly in a canal boat and that the above information and accompanying tables etc, offer only the minimum of background details.

Useful Addresses and Telephone Nos

Dockmaster
The Watch House
Cumberland Basin Lock Entrance
Brunel Lock Road
Bristol BS1 6XG
Tel: Bristol (0117) 927 3633

Dues Clerk
Harbour Office
Underfall Yard
Cumberland Road
Bristol BS1 6XG
Tel: Bristol (0117) 926 4797 or 929 7608

Harbour Master
Underfall Yard
Cumberland Road
Bristol BS1 6XG
Tel: Bristol (0117) 926 4797 or 929 7608

British Waterways
The Pier Head
Sharpness Docks
Dursley
Tel: (Dursley) (01453) 511862
(normally during office hours only)

Harbour Master
Sharpness Docks
Sharpness
Tel: (Thornbury) 01454 811862 (from 5 hours before until 1 hour after high water)

Marinecall Weather
Tel: 0891 500459

Pilotage
From/to Sharpness
Tel: 0374 226143

River Avon
The Pilots' Office
Haven Master's Building
Royal Edward Dock
Avonmouth BS11 9AT
Tel: Bristol (0117) 982 3081

Pleasure Craft Locking Schedule
(Bristol Docks, Entrance Lock)

	Times before High Water	
	Outward	Inward
	hrs mins	hrs mins
1st locking	2 50	2 35
2nd locking	1 40	1 25
3rd locking	30	15

A Cumberland Basin Tide Table can be obtained from the Harbour Master's Office at Bristol.

Charts and Guides
Admiralty Charts are available from:
W.F. Price & Co
Wapping Wharf
Bristol BS1 6UD
Tel: Bristol (0117) 929 2229
Charts 1166 (Avonmouth to Sharpness and 1859 (River Avon) apply.

Bristol Harbour: Information for Boat Owners – available from the Harbour Master's Office at Bristol.

Trip-Boats

For many, an outing on a trip-boat is their first encounter with the magic of canals; for some the experience is to change a mild interest into an obsession. As a result of the fragmentation that restoration begat, there are more trip-boats on the K&A than any other comparable navigation.

KENNET CRUISES, 14 Beech Lane, Earley, Reading RG6 5PT; tel: (0118) 959 0346 or (0831) 326482. Up to 48 passengers in *Lancing* from Burghfield Bridge; charter and public trips.

KENNET HORSE BOAT CO, 32 West Mills, Newbury RG14 5HU; tel: (01635) 44154. Up to 90 passengers in motor barge *Avon* from Newbury; charter and public trips.

KENNET HORSE BOAT CO, (see above). Up to 75 passengers in horse-drawn *Kennet Valley* from Kintbury; charter and public trips.

KENNET & AVON CANAL TRUST, c/o Bob Maslin; tel: (01488) 683389. Up to 50 passengers in *Rose of Hungerford* from Hungerford; charter and public trips.

PEWSEY VALE CHARTER CRUISES, 239 Leigh Road, Chandlers Ford, Hants SO53 3AX; tel: (01703) 266200 or 0831 807196. Up to 57 passengers in *Sarah Davey* from Wootton Rivers or Pewsey Wharf; charter and public trips.

KENNET & AVON CANAL TRUST, c/o Jackie Roff; tel: (01672) 564864. Up to 12 passengers in *Dragonfly* from Pewsey Wharf; charter and public trips.

GIBSONS BOAT SERVICES, Old Builder's Wharf, Honeystreet, Wiltshire SN9 5PS; tel: (01672) 851232. Up to 12 passengers in electric-powered *Patricia II*; charter.

WHITE HORSE BOATS, 8 Southgate Close, Devizes SN10 5AQ; tel: (01380) 728504. Up to 50 passengers in *Kenavon Venture* from Horton and Devizes; charter and public trips.

KENNET & AVON CANAL TRUST; tel: (01225) 868683. Up to 40 passengers in *Ladywood* from Bradford-on-Avon; charter and public trips.

KENNET & AVON CANAL TRUST, c/o Janet Williams; tel: (01225) 462313. Up to 44 passengers in *Jubilee* from Dundas; charter and public trips.

JOHN RENNIE CANAL CRUISES, Sydney Wharf, Bathwick Hill, Bath BA2 4EL; tel: (01225) 447276. Up to 60 passengers in *John Rennie* from Bath; charter and public trips.

AVON LEISURE, 4 Thomas Street, Bath; tel: (01225) 333769. Up to 120 passengers in *Pride of Bath* from below North Parade Bridge, Bath; charter and public trips.

BRISTOL AND BATH CRUISERS, Phoenix Wharf, Bristol; tel: (0117) 9214307/657985/(01454) 311580. Up to 66 passengers in *Flower of Bristol* and *Enterprise of Bristol* in Floating Harbour and on River Avon; charter and public trips (eves).

BRISTOL PACKET, Wapping Wharf, Bristol BS1 6UN; tel: (0117) 9268157/735315. Up to 127 passengers in *Tower Belle* and 54 in *Redshank* in Floating Harbour and on River Avon; charter and public trips.

All trip-boat locations are indicated by ⬚t on the relevant map.

Hotel Boats

WILLOW WREN CRUISING HOLIDAYS, PO Box 2, Rugby, Warwickshire CV21 1TD; tel: (01788) 569153. Up to 10 passengers in *Tsarina & Tsarevna* and 9 on *Tranquil Rose* from Newbury, Pewsey, Bradford-on-Avon and Bath.

HOTELBOAT HARLEQUIN LTD, Hilperton Wharf, Trowbridge, Wiltshire BA14 8RS; tel: 0403 218239. Up to 10 passengers in broad-beam *Harlequin* between Devizes and Bristol.

INLAND WATERWAYS HOLIDAY CRUISES, Greenham Lock Cottage, London Road, Newbury, Berkshire RG14 5SN; tel: 0831 110811. Up to 9 passengers in *Snipe* and *Taurus* along the length of the canal.

HOTEL BOAT HELEN OF THE WEST, PO Box 937, Devizes, Wiltshire SN10 3TG; tel: (07971) 599 379. Up to 4 passengers for weekends or B&B in the week in *Helen of the West* from Devizes east along the Long Pound.

All hotel boat locations are indicated by ⬚h on the relevant map.

General Information

Maximum Navigable Dimensions

Reading to Bath
Length   72ft
Beam   13ft 2ins
(For *broad-beam craft* the maximum length is 70ft)
Draught   3ft
Headroom   7ft
Note: Higher-than-normal fresh water levels on the river Kennet occasionally reduce headroom, particularly at Reading, though boaters are advised not to be cruising in such conditions.
Bath to Bristol
Length   75ft
Beam   16ft
Draught   3ft
Headroom   8ft 9ins
Note: Draught can be reduced to nearer 3ft at Hanham Lock when the river Avon is running low.
Note: Headroom for craft with a beam of 10ft or more could be reduced by 1ft by the low haunches of White Hart Bridge at Keynsham.
Note: Excessive fresh water levels and/or tidal influences may effect headroom on the Avon, particularly at Churchill Bridge, Bath.

Licences

Reading to Hanham (BW)
Private craft normally based on BW waters should display a licence; details of prices, etc, are available from British Waterways, Willow Grange, Church Road, Watford WD1 3QA; tel: Watford (01923) 226422.
Hanham to Bristol (Bristol City Docks)
Private craft normally moored in Bristol City Docks' waters should display a licence; details of prices, etc, are available from the Dues Clerk, City Docks, Underfall Yard, Cumberland Road, Bristol BS1 6XG; tel: Bristol (0117) 926 4797 or 9297608.
Short term licences can be obtained at Hanham Lock (BW and Bristol City Docks), tel: Bristol (0117) 986 2550, at Netham Lock (Bristol City Docks only), tel: Bristol (0117) 977 6590 and from Reading Marine Co (BW only), tel: Reading (01734) 573917.
Craft 'slipped' onto the canal can obtain short-term licences at the above as well as from Newbury Boat Co, Devizes Wharf, tranquil boats at Semington, Bradford Wharf and Bath Locks.
Craft leaving the Kennet for the Thames will require a Thames visitor's licence; these are available from National Rivers Authority, PO Box 214, Reading RG1 8HQ; tel: Reading (01734) 535650.
Hire boats are normally only licenced for their 'home' waters; to stray beyond may well require the purchase of a short-term licence.

Useful Addresses

British Waterways (Southern Region)
Willow Grange
Church Road
Watford WD1 3QA
Tel: Watford (01923) 208700

British Waterways (K&A Canal Office)
The Locks
Bath Road
Devizes SN10 1HB
Tel: Devizes (01380) 722859

Harbour Master Bristol Docks
Harbour Master's Office
Underfall Yard
Cumberland Road
Bristol BS1 6XG
Tel: Bristol (0117) 926 4797 or 929 7608

Emergencies

To contact British Waterways in an emergency, phone 100 and ask for *Freephone Canals*; mobile phone users call 01384 215785.

Canal Closures

On the assumption that boating is a seasonal activity, canals and rivers are normally maintained between November and Easter. Such closures that result are well publicised in the waterways press (see below) and information is available from local BW offices. In addition BW's Canalphone South, 01923 201402, delivers recorded details though, clearly, unscheduled stoppages may not be included; boatyards normally have the most up-to-date information. The walker is rarely disrupted by such closures.

Waterways Pressure Groups

The *Kennet & Avon Canal Trust* has been at the forefront of the restoration of the Kennet & Avon for over a quarter of a century. To get involved in the Trust and its work contact: K&ACT, Canal Centre, Couch Lane, Devizes SN10 1EB. Tel: (01380) 721279.

The *Wilts & Berks Canal Amenity Group* was formed in the 70s to stem the tide of deterioration on the canal and restore as much as possible for local amenity use. The Group can be contacted at 8 Raymond Road, Maidenhead SL6 6DF; tel: (01628) 544666.

The *Association of Canal Enterprises* was formed in the early 80s as an association of those involved commercially on the canal and today has 30 members. For further information (especially details of new enterprises not included in this guide) contact the Association at Greenham Lock Cottage, London Road, Newbury RG14 5SN; tel: (01635) 42884.

The *Inland Waterways Association* is a national organisation with local branches, originally created in the late 1940s to campaign for the reclamation of Britain's inland waterways network. Membership details from IWA, PO Box 114, Rickmansworth WD3 1ZY; tel: (01923) 711114.

Waterways Magazines & Journals

Waterways World: national monthly magazine
Canal & Riverboat: national monthly magazine
Canal Boat and Inland Waterways: national monthly magazine
Motor Boat & Yachting: national monthly magazine
Waterways: IWA quarterly magazine
The Butty: K&ACT quarterly publication

Bibliography

Images of the Kennet & Avon: 100 Years in Camera by Niall Allsop
Pubs on the Kennet & Avon Canal by Niall Allsop
The Somersetshire Coal Canal Rediscovered by Niall Allsop
The Kennet & Avon Canal by Kenneth R Clew
Wessex Waterway by Kenneth R Clew
The Kennet & Avon Canal: A Journey from Newbury to Bath in 1964 by John Russell
The Floating Harbour: A Landscape History of the Bristol City Docks by John Lord and Jem Southam
Avon Villages by Edmund J Mason and Dorrien Mason
Wiltshire Villages by Brian J Woodruffe
Companion into Berkshire by R P Beckinsale
Bristol Brass: The History of the Industry by Joan Day
Landscape with Canals by L T C Rolt
Britain's Lost Waterways by Michael E Ware
Through England's Waterways by Montague and Ann Lloyd
The Strange Adventures of a Houseboat by William Black
Kennet & Avon Canal Trust's *Towpath Guides*
Kennet & Avon Waterway, Eastern and Western Charts by Nicholas Hammond
The Canal Age by Charles Hadfield
Navigable Waterways by L T C Rolt
Shell Book of Inland Waterways by Hugh McKnight
Narrow Boat by L T C Rolt
Bread Upon The Waters by David Blagrove
Exploring the Kennet & Avon Canal by Nigel Vile
GEOprojects' map *The Kennet & Avon Canal*

Lock Names

1	Hanham	66	Potters
2	Keynsham	67	Little Bedwyn
3	Swineford	68	Oakhill Down
4	Saltford	69	Froxfield Middle
5	Kelston	70	Froxfield Bottom
6	Weston	71	Picketfield
7	Bath Lower or Bottom	72	Cobbler's
8/9	Bath Deep	73	Hungerford Marsh
10	Wash House	74	Hungerford
11	Rasamar or Abbey View	75	Dunmill
12	Second or Pulteney	76	Wire
13	Bath Top	77	Brunsden's
(7-13	Bath or Widcombe Flight)	78	Kintbury
14	Bradford	79	Dreweat's
15	Buckley's or Semington Bottom	80	Copse
16	Barrett's or Semington Top	81	Hamstead
17-21	Seend Locks	82	Benham
22	Fundraisers'	83	Higg's
23-37	Devizes Locks	84	Guyer's
38	Jack Dolby	85	Newbury
39	Skaggs Foundation	86	Greenham
40	Paul Ensor	87	Ham
41	Boto-X	88	Bull's
42	Monument	89	Widmead
43	Queen Elizabeth II	90	Monkey Marsh
44	Sir Hugh Stockwell	91	Colthrop
45	Cave	92	Midgham
46	A P Herbert	93	Heale's
47	Manifold	94	Woolhampton
48	Trust	95	Aldermaston
49	Maton	96	Padworth
50	Kennet	97	Towney
(22-50	Devizes Flight)	(98	Ufton – degated)
51	Wootton Rivers	99	Tyle Mill
52	Heathy Close	100	Sulhamstead
53	Brimslade	101	Sheffield
54	Cadley	102	Garston
(51-54	Wootton Rivers Flight)	103	Burghfield
55-63	Crofton Locks	104	Southcote
64	Bedwyn Church	105	Fobney
65	Burnt Mill	106	County

opposite: Time for a break at Little Bedwyn Lock

— The Boating Bit:
Constructive advice for the inland boater, novice or otherwise, including tips for making the most of cruising on the Kennet & Avon ▬

Setting Off
Knowing that your boat is waterway-worthy is no less important than being sure that your car won't let you down on the motorway. Reputable hire-bases will furnish you with details of what daily checks to carry out to ensure trouble-free boating. This will vary from base to base, and boat to boat but the following, which, like most of the advice on these pages, is directed towards the steerer, might be useful.
• Check that all your boat's 'services' are as they should be – full water tank, sufficient gas, empty loo, empty rubbish bin – you might not be able to do anything there and then, but if you know what needs to be done it will help you plan your day's boating.
• Check that the stern-tube greaser has been tightened – best done *after* a day's cruising but still worth checking before setting off.
• Check the engine's oil level on the dipstick.
• Check engine coolant levels where applicable.
• Ensure that the gear lever is disengaged or in neutral before starting the engine.

Now that you're ready for the 'off', bear the following in mind:
• Ensure that, after untying the boat, all mooring pins are withdrawn and brought aboard, and that no ropes are dangling overboard; in addition, the latter should always be stored tidily, as in an emergency a tangled rope can be a serious handicap.
• Before pulling out into the channel, make sure it is safe to do so – pushing the bank with a shaft from the bows (the sharp end!) will get you cleanly underway.
• As a canal or river is normally much shallower by its banks, use the throttle lightly to get under way – a furiously-rotating propeller only churns up mud and hinders progress.

Steering
No apologies for stating the obvious: the tiller is pushed to the left to turn the boat right and right to turn the boat to the left. But bear in mind the following:
• The boat's stern (the blunt end!) sits lowest in the water so try to keep it in the deepest part of the channel – usually the centre.
• The 'rule of the road' is *keep right* – the opposite to driving on the highway. This is normally only applicable to passing approaching craft.

• There is no need to give approaching craft too wide a berth; to do so in a narrow channel is to risk running aground. Instead, aim to keep just right of centre and, having eased off the throttle, pass such craft with no more than two feet to spare. (Experienced boaters will get it right down to inches.) When both boats are alongside start to steer the bows back to the centre of the channel.
• Strong cross-winds can be a boating nightmare and in open stretches will try to wrestle control of the boat from the steerer. Allow for such conditions when steering and be aware that trees, bridges and locks can suddenly alter whatever effect the wind is having.
• Keep a weather-eye open for any gushing flow of water into the main channel that might directionally affect the boat, and compensate by steering into it.
• Most canal craft do not steer well in reverse, the exception being those with outboard motors. Should such a situation be unavoidable, the following should be borne in mind: in whichever direction the bend at the back of the tiller is pointing is the direction that the stern will tend to go – if the boat does not respond, short bursts of forward will compensate, as will the pushing power of a member of crew at the bows with a shaft.
• If you lose steerage, fail to make any headway under apparently normal conditions or are aware of a 'foamy' wash coming up from the propeller, then it is likely that there is a foreign body wound round the propeller. Tie up safely and remove the offending article(s) via the weed hatch, making sure first of all that the engine is switched off and, if applicable, that any starting key is withdrawn.
Make sure the weed-hatch is replaced.

Speed
The maximum speed permissible on most BW waterways is 4mph, equivalent to a brisk walking pace. Such a figure is meaningless on most shallow inland navigations and boaters should keep to much lower speeds using the following as their guidelines:
• If you are making any sort of wave behind the boat, then you are going too fast.
• If you are making a wave that breaks on the bank you are going too fast.
• Slow down passing all moored craft – you'll know why if you're moored up yourself and another boat speeds by.
• Slow down passing all BW maintenance craft.

• Slow down passing fishermen.
• Slow down means down to 'tickover' speed.

On the Kennet & Avon
• Boats are only likely to achieve the 4mph maximum on the river Avon and on the Feeder Canal where it is also the limit.

• The limit in the Floating Harbour is 6mph, though the restrictions to speed already outlined are still applicable.

Turning
For short craft (30ft or less) there is normally no shortage of places to turn. The crew of longer boats will have to use their own judgment, while the longest craft will need to seek out a junction, a boatyard or a winding hole. (Paradoxically 'winding' is pronounced as in 'blow' not as in 'turn'.)
• To turn in a winding hole, put the bows into the 'hole' – invariably the non-towpath side – which keeps the stern in the deepest water. With timely bursts of forward and reverse the boat can easily be swung round; some boaters prefer to *gently* run the bows aground, and keeping the throttle in forward and the tiller hard over, swing the stern round before reversing off and forward whence they came.

On the Kennet & Avon
• Even the longest craft will find they can turn almost anywhere on the river Avon; in fast-flowing conditions, crews should not underestimate the power of the current to push a boat downstream broadside.

• On the Kennet it is normally possible to turn where river and canal separate or rejoin, though an awareness of the potential force of the flow would not go amiss.

Running Aground
This occurs most frequently when passing other craft or when the steerer starts to indulge in a bit of prolonged sightseeing:
• Assuming there is no danger to other craft, remedy the situation by going into

opposite: Waves and wildlife at West Mills Swing Bridge, Newbury

reverse which will normally draw the stern of the boat into deeper water.
• If you're well and truly stuck, don't fight it by repeatedly revving the engine. Stop and think. If you know where the boat is grounded, move the crew as far from that point as possible and try reversing – but *not* full throttle. If you're still stuck, push the stern out into deeper water using poles or shafts; hopefully too the bows will disengage if also aground. When going forward try not to steer yourself back aground!

Swing and Lift Bridges
As with locks, the operation of all moveable bridges is the more efficient for a little planning ahead.
• Follow all instructions attached to any such bridge and never assume they all work the same way.
• Most bridges have some sort of fixing; ascertain what and where this is but do not undo it until the bridge is clear of pedestrians and traffic. Be sure to replace any fixings once the bridge is closed.
• In the interests of safety keep all crew off the roof of the boat.
• Never start to close a swing bridge or lower a lift bridge until the boat is through; if another boat is approaching, bridges may be left open provided this can be done safely.

Locks and Locking
One of the mysteries of life? Not so … it's all fairly logical and straightforward and, should you be hiring a boat for the first time, something that all hire-bases should instruct

you in and demonstrate if possible. The principles are these:
• A lock is a step up or a step down, necessary as sloping water – usually called a weir or waterfall – is definitely *not* navigable!

• If, at a lock, the water therein is not at the same level as you and your boat, then it must be made so before you can go any further.
• To raise the water level in a lock water can only be drawn off the higher of the two canal levels by winding up the paddles *at that end of the lock*.
• To lower the water level in a lock it has to be emptied into the lower canal level by winding up the paddles *at that end of the lock* and letting the water out.
• The same principles are used to alter the levels when a boat is in the lock.
• No gates will open until the level on both sides is the same.
• Only the paddles at *one* end should ever be raised at the same time – to have them all raised is to risk draining the higher level and flooding the lower.

Having mastered the theory, the following tips should make life easier:
• Think ahead. This guide shows exactly where each lock is so it makes sense to send crew ahead (they can normally step off at a preceding bridge) to get things ready.
• If the lock is set against you, don't start changing things until you are sure that no other boat is approaching from the opposite direction – it makes sense to let them go first and it will save thousands of gallons of water.
• If there is room, share locks with other boats whenever possible – it lightens the work load and saves water. If a steel boat and a glass-fibre boat are to share a lock

end-on then the steel boat should be in front.
• Set about working the lock slowly and methodically – don't raise any paddles until the gates at the other end are closed and its adjacent paddles have been wound down – and never rush around or near the edge of the chamber.
• When filling a lock with boats in it, open the paddles a little at a time, as to do otherwise is likely to cause a problem for the boats.
• Never leave a windlass on the paddle spindle – if the paddle were to slip it could spin off and cause serious injury.
• Never wind down the paddles until the gates are open – but make sure that they are wound down *before* you leave.
• Unless otherwise instructed, close all lock gates behind you – the only exception being if another boat is approaching or already waiting to use the lock.
• Normally, narrow boats using wide locks need only have to open one of the gates.
• Check that you have still got your windlass – and your crew – with you before heading on.
• Where locks are closely grouped, it makes sense for crews to distribute their energies in such a way as to make efficient progress through the locks; for example, someone could be preparing ahead and someone 'closing down' behind.

Tunnels

As tunnel roofs have a tendency to leak, wear a mac ... though the following are more important.
• Switch on the boat's headlight before entering a tunnel and switch it off after leaving.
• Keep all crew members off the boat's roof.
• Children are safer *inside* – an accident in the dark depths of a tunnel could have disastrous consequences.

On the Kennet & Avon
• For narrow-beam craft (7ft or less) Bruce Tunnel is two-way.

Mooring

In an emergency, mooring is possible almost anywhere on a canal or river but in normal circumstances some places are better than others.
• Do not moor on the non-towpath side unless at specified boatyard or pub moorings.
• Don't moor on tight bends, in winding holes, at junctions, at water or similar service points (unless using them), close to bridges or locks, in a lock flight or in a particularly narrow channel.
• On a river always moor facing upstream, even if this means turning.

Having chosen your spot, proceed as follows:
• Slow down as you approach in preparation for swinging the bows in; a boat cannot be reversed into a mooring space as if it were a car. Remember, too, that in a river the flow will act as a potential brake.
• Bring the bows into the bank and stop (by engaging reverse and then neutral) close enough for a member of crew to step off with the bow rope. If there is only one crew member then he or she should either keep in touch with the bow rope or tie it to something before being thrown the stern rope to pull the boat in. If all this takes time do not be intimidated by other boaters whom you might be momentarily delaying.
• If, due to shallow water, one end of the boat has to 'stick out' then this should preferably be the stern; a plank for getting on and off will be needed in such circumstances.
• Never tie ropes *across* the towpath – they would be an obvious danger to walkers.
• Insert mooring pins at an angle sloping away from the boat and positioned at angles either going away from or inwards from the bows and stern.
• Tie something bright or white to the ends of mooring pins if they are likely to be a hazard to walkers.
• Having 'engaged' the mooring pin or bollard, return the mooring ropes to the boat.

Rivers

Most of the preceding information is equally relevant to river cruising though moving water does have its own distinctive attributes.
• Keep to the outside of bends whenever possible where the water is always deeper – but keep an eye open for oncoming craft doing exactly the same.
• River water moves ... and will thus effect any manoeuvre you make, particularly turning and stopping.
• Remember that progress upstream will be slower than downstream.
• Always moor facing upstream; clearly this might involve turning, but it's worth the inconvenience.
• River levels can rise (or fall) quite dramatically; if you have to be on a river in such conditions then moor with longer ropes than usual to allow for any rise (or fall).
• Always carry an anchor on board – rigged and easily accessible. Engines don't only stall on canals and if the flow is pulling you towards potential danger, an anchor is your only brake!

Crews and Children

It is a sad reflection on the ways of the world that most pleasure boats seem to be under the control of a male steerer. There is no reason why this should be so ... other, that is, than the almost instinctive attitude that it should be so and a tendency for some women to be machine-shy. This is no mere sexist propaganda for there is the serious point that situations can arise wherein it might be important, even vital, that a second member of the crew should have the ability and confidence to assume control. All too often the typical hire-base scenario sees 'Dad' being shown how to start, steer and stop while 'Mum' is getting the hang of the cooker, fridge and a new-fangled appliance – the windlass!

Children too are often under-estimated. With the right sort of instruction they can turn their hand to almost anything – from steering (under supervision) to working locks – that is within their physical abilities and/or intellectual grasp. If nothing else, inland boating is an activity in which all the family can and should participate.

Finally, whatever your fashion sense, make sure that children wear life-jackets whenever you're under way and that you and all members of crew are decked out in non-slip footwear ... you can always dress up for the pub in the evening!

On the Kennet & Avon
• Even in summer the Avon is prone to flash-flooding so try to keep abreast of local weather conditions; heavy and prolonged rainfall in North Wiltshire will take about 36hrs to make a nuisance of itself at Bath ... add to this the occasional tidal 'barrier' at Hanham and you have a recipe for a rapid rise in the river's level. On the plus side no part of the Avon is more than three hours cruising from still waters ... so it's all just a matter of common sense.

• Between Hanham and Netham, the Avon is also under tidal influence; the normal downstream flow of the river can thus be 'adjusted' by an incoming tidal flow or its ebb.

• Don't try to turn on the Avon just upstream of any of its bridges which have a central (midstream) pier – a boat drifting broadside downstream might damage it!

• Boats mooring on the Avon by Bath's Pulteney Weir are advised to add to their security by tying up (at the bows) with a length of lockable (and adjustable) chain. It is not unknown hereabouts for mooring ropes to be cut as part of the night's 'festivities' and chain is more resistant to the pocket knife.

• The Kennet may appear to be a placid, almost canal-like navigation but, like the Avon, it has its moments, however infrequent. Boaters are advised not to be seduced into complacency by its meandering rural charms.

• The traffic-light controlled Brewery Gut forces the Kennet into a narrower channel than it would like – the flow is thus faster and should not be under-estimated.

Six Walks

The Kennet & Avon Canal is, of course, a linear walk in itself: but it is only by occasionally leaving the waterside path that it can be put into its environmental and historical context. The six walks described in the following pages are an attempt to do just that. They do not necessarily traverse the most picturesque terrain or explore the most historically 'alive' parts of the navigation's environs; they are however all legal, exhilarating, circular … and fun.

All start on the waterway where boaters and walkers using this guide might well be anyway, though each is also accessible by car and public transport – however infrequent. No special clothing or footwear is necessary, all six walks having been 'tested' during the muddy depths of winter in, among other things, a pair of wellies.

As can be seen from the map below, the walks are well spaced out throughout the length of the canal and as such offer very differing views of the Kennet & Avon and its landscape. Walks 1 & 2 – Bristol's Floating Harbour and the Bradford-on-Avon/Avoncliff area – are dominated by the river Avon, encapsulated as a huge, tame inner-city amenity on the one hand and as an unnavigable, but beautiful, obstacle on the other. Walks 5 & 6 – around Marsh Benham and Aldermaston – are about the river Kennet, the embryonic strength of its earliest encounters with the

navigation contrasting with its assertiveness as the mainstay of the old Kennet Navigation east of Newbury. And in between, on either side of the canal's summit, Walks 3 & 4 – in and around Honeystreet and between Great Bedwyn and Crofton – are examples of pure canal as, on the one hand, it wanders lock-less through the ancient Vale of Pewsey and, on the other, consumes lock-full after lock-full of water from the summit reservoir at Wilton.

The description of each walk has three basic elements – **directions**, fertile ramblings and observations and *features of special interest* – the style of print indicating which is which. The numbers and letters that precede the directions and special features correspond respectively to numbers and letters on the maps. In addition there are details of where to refuel the tired body, and, for the tireless, suggestions for adding on a few extra miles. Telephone numbers of local public transport services and Tourist Information Centres are also included.

The maps are drawn to various scales, though each is proportionally accurate; the bolder lines indicate the route as described though any road track or path marked may offer an alternative. As explained above, changes in direction are numbered and relate to numbers in the text while special features are labelled alphabetically and also tie in with the text. Finally, these are no 'armchair' walks. They are included in the hope, even expectation, that the reader will venture 'out there' to enjoy – and respect – the navigation's architectural, industrial, agricultural and natural environment.

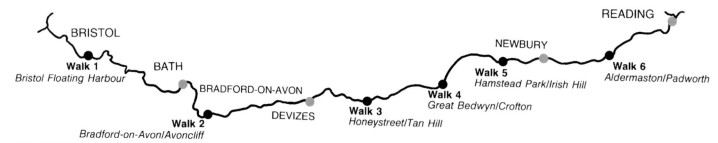

BRISTOL

Walk 1
Bristol Floating Harbour

BATH

BRADFORD-ON-AVON

Walk 2
Bradford-on-Avon/Avoncliff

DEVIZES

Walk 3
Honeystreet/Tan Hill

Walk 4
Great Bedwyn/Crofton

NEWBURY

Walk 5
Hamstead Park/Irish Hill

READING

Walk 6
Aldermaston/Padworth

Walk 1   4½ Miles

Start: Bristol Bridge   OS ref: ST 590729

Bristol's floating harbour is a unique inner-city amenity; there is so much to see that, including a few stops for sustenance, this walk could take all day.

1   Proceed along the waterfront, south from Bristol Bridge.

In one sense the Bristol Bridge area is the key to the city's maritime past for it was here that the river Frome originally joined the Avon. The 13th-century re-routing of the Frome (to join the Avon at what is now the Arnolfini area) gave the Bristol side of the river distinct advantages over the rival Redcliffe side … all of which is a far cry from the floating restaurants and bars and the large – though not incompatible – office complexes that line today's quay walls.

2   Turn right into King Street

A   KING STREET was originally laid out in 1663 and survives today not only as the custodian of a variety of architectural styles but also as the home of some fine pubs and restaurants, notably the Llandoger Trow,

believed to be the Admiral Benbow in Stevenson's Treasure Island and opposite, the Old Duke of live-jazz fame. Here too is Britain's oldest continuously working theatre, Bristol Old Vic, opened in 1766 and flanked today by the 17th-century St Nicholas Almshouse and 19th-century warehousing.

3   Turn sharp left and walk down through Queen Square.

Walking along the busy thoroughfare that bisects Queen Square it is difficult to recreate the genteel scene that these fashionable terraces once oversaw. Many of the original buildings were victims of the 1831 Reform riots though some remain, particularly along the south side … perhaps the greatest destruction occurred during the 1930s when 20th-century Man cut a diagonal swathe through the square in praise of the motor car. Like the *Llandoger Trow*, the *Hole in the Wall* begs to be considered in the *Treasure Island* Look-a-like Competition … this time as the model for The Spyglass.

4   Cross the road and turn right round the *Hole in the Wall* and along the waterfront.

5   At the T-junction cross Prince Street, turning left

and then right round the Arnolfini to Narrow Quay, continuing round the top of St Augustine's Reach and down the other side, past the old Transit Sheds.

B   ST AUGUSTINE'S REACH is the remaining unculverted length of the river Frome and its re-routed confluence with the Avon. The diversionary trench was cut in the 1240s and, until the 1890s, extended for another ¼ mile northwards. As the Frome was progressively culverted the tall masts became victims of the internal combustion engine. Back in the 13th century there was no 'Float' and the Reach was still tidal; nevertheless the 120ft wide and 18ft deep channel offered, at the time, almost unrivalled facilities, capable of handling the largest craft of the day. The 'diversion' of the Frome not only brought distinct trading advantages to Bristol but also altered considerably the town's topography and thus its future development.

Besides the various revitalised warehousing and the new, and generally complementary, buildings, it is the massive mooring bollards and rings set in cobbles that recreate images of tall ships and cranes, their giant cobwebs of rigging stretching skywards. Neptune's statue has only overseen this truncated version of the Reach since 1949 … though he had lived in the Temple part of the city since 1723. Like Neptune, the ornate weathervane, on the corner in front of the new Lloyds Building and its semi-circular amphitheatre, was rescued from another part of the city and scarcely looks out of place in its new setting atop the base of an old steam crane. Between these two 'newcomers' is the magnificent Watershed complex, a fine example of how redundant dock buildings can be given a new lease of life.

6　At the 'dead end' cross the cobbled road, on the right and follow the lane on the left (keeping the stone wall on your right) towards the brick chimney; continue round to the right to the main road.

7　Turn left onto the main road and keep left at the roundabout, cutting back to the waterfront opposite the *SS Great Britain* and the *Matthew*; continue along waterfront as far as the *Pumphouse*.

It is a feature of this walk that almost everything has two perspectives – one seen from alongside and one from across the Harbour. There are exceptions as, from time to time, the waterfront route is 'blocked' by some commercial or recreational activity ... though what is missed is eventually visible from 'over there'. The *SS Great Britain* and the *Matthew* replica are cases in point; the view of the former, standing proudly in the dock that bore it, contrasts dramatically with the occasional glimpse of its masts from the other side. The view of the *Matthew* is the only one you'll get without paying!

C　HOTWELL DOCK is an 18th-century, pre-Floating Harbour attempt at improving the city's docks and ironically, remains as the Harbour's only surviving commercial operation. Sand dredged from the Bristol Channel is brought up-river to the Dock for eventual distribution to the local building trade. Alongside the Dock, atop the erstwhile Merchant's Dock, is the tasteful modern development of Rownham Mead, one of several that contribute to the overall 'living-working-playing' ethos that the Harbour now exudes.

8　Turn left onto the main road and cross the Merchant's Road Swing Bridge towards the *Nova Scotia*, continuing with its sweep round to the left to join Cumberland Road; remain on this road until the *Cottage's* pub sign.

D　CUMBERLAND BASIN is the name given to the area between Merchant's Road Swing Bridge and the Harbour's Entrance Lock; it is an area that, modern roads notwithstanding, has seen some subtle changes since the Harbour's completion in 1809. Originally there were two locking systems – two Entrance Locks into Cumberland Basin from the river and a Junction Lock from the Basin into the Harbour. The earliest docks were designed by Jessop (1804-1809), one of which was improved by Brunel (1844-1849) before Thomas Howard (1867-1873) added to and improved

the whole system. The swing bridge spans two chambers, both now redundant – the northern one being Howard's and the southern Jessop's Junction Lock. To the west the new Plimsoll Bridge spans Howard's Entrance Lock – the only one still in use – while to the south are the remains of Jessop's two Entrance Locks, in the most southerly of which Brunel assisted. Most of these changes were to accommodate larger vessels, inevitably a losing battle as the meandering Avon ultimately presented more natural restrictions. Ironically too it was engineers like Brunel who, by building larger ships, hastened the maritime demise of Bristol.

Everywhere you look there is so much to see: Hotwell's terraces tumble down the hillside while below Cumberland Road, like a rejected child, is the forlorn channel of the New Cut; Clifton Suspension Bridge penetrates the skyline, an ever-present monument to Brunel's genius while atop Brandon Hill stands Cabot Tower, built in 1897 to commemorate the 400th anniversary of John Cabot's voyage of discovery.

9　Turn left towards the *Cottage* and turn right at the pub along the waterfront.

10　Bear right at the marina, following the waterside round to the road, turn right and take the first left down the side of Bristol Diving School; turn left again and head back down to the water and *SS Great Britain*; turn right and continue along waterfront.

E　The SS GREAT BRITAIN was designed by Brunel, launched in 1843, saw service in the Crimean War, was beached and left to rust off the Falkland Islands, returned to Bristol in 1970 ... a potted history that scarcely does justice to the colourful and dramatic story of such a ship – the first to embody all the new technologies of the time – iron construction, steam power and screw propulsion. It is a fitting thought that the Great Britain should return to its birthplace for its final fit-out. The replica of John Cabot's Matthew is now part of the Great Britain 'experience'.

11　Cross the main road by Prince Street Swing Bridge and follow the water's edge to and round Bathurst Basin.

The old Wapping and Princes Wharves are the place for living history. Alongside the *Great Britain* and the *Matthew* there's the new Maritime Heritage Centre which takes a special

look at boatbuilding at Bristol. At the other end there's the National Lifeboat Museum and the Bristol Industrial Museum and, linking the two, *Henbury*, a steam locomotive built in 1937 ... and, of course, there's the Fairbairn Steam Crane built by Bath's Stothert & Pitt in 1875.

The 'organised' past soon gives way to the more 'natural' variety in the shape of Bathurst Basin, originally one of three entrances into the Floating Harbour from the New Cut. The housing along Bathurst Parade is a tasteful blend of old and new, representatives of two styles and eras which, like the *Ostrich* and the Hospital opposite, are entirely compatible.

12　Turn right onto Phoenix (formerly Midland) Wharf and then up the 'Donkey Ramp' at the end, turning left onto the road.

Beyond Phoenix is Redcliffe Wharf, an interesting feature of which is its caves which probably have their origins in the extraction of sand for ballast. Other industrial and storage uses followed and some were eventually filled in, taking with them perhaps some of their secrets including the long-held belief that an underground passage linked the wharf with the crypt off St Mary Redcliffe.

13　Follow Redcliffe Parade East down towards the church, turn left on to the main road and cross it at the crossing, turning left to cross Redcliffe Bridge.

F　ST MARY REDCLIFFE was described by Elizabeth I as the " fairest, goodliest and most famous parish church in England" ... and this despite the fact that it had been virtually spireless since 1446 when it was struck by lightning. Originally a 12th-century chapel in the extensive parish of Bedminster, St Mary Redcliffe grew in size and stature until the late 14th century by which time, apart from the spire, it looked much as it does today. The new spire was erected in the 1870s, its crowning glory no less matched by its magnificent interior.

14　Turn right down Welsh Back towards Bristol Bridge.

The walk along Welsh Back – so-named after the coastal trade with Wales – brings to an end what can only be a whistle-stop tour of Bristol's Floating Harbour ... the over-riding impression left is of relief that the call to 'fill it in' was ignored. The uncertainty of the 70s has given way to the pride of the 80s with the Harbour's past, present and future assured of a place in the 90s and beyond.

SUSTENANCE: There is scarcely more than a few hundred yards without an inviting watering-hole.

... AND THERE'S MORE: The walk can easily be extended in both directions – westwards (following the Avon Walkway signs) along the Avon's southern shore to Pill from where a return bus can be caught; eastwards to take in Castle Park and some of the city's earliest history.

PUBLIC TRANSPORT: Bristol has excellent local and national rail and road connections; train details from Bristol (0117) 929 4255 and bus information from (0117) 955 3231. A ferry service operates in the Floating Harbour, details from Bristol (0117) 955 8986.

TOURIST INFORMATION CENTRE: St Nicholas Church, St Nicholas Street, Bristol. Tel: Bristol (0117) 927 3416.

Walk 2   3¼ Miles

Start: Bradford Lock Bridge   OS ref: ST 826603

It is in the Bradford-on-Avon area that the canal has its first encounter with the river Avon; This walk captures the flavour of their parallel course and the drama of their first confrontation.

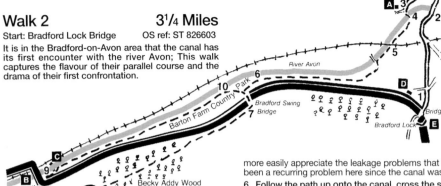

1 Proceed north from Bradford Lock Bridge towards the town.

The erstwhile wool town of Bradford-on-Avon clings to the Avon's steep-sided valley with some of its oldest buildings clustering round the river crossing, the 'broad ford' that gave it its name. The entrance to the ford can be seen on the western side of its replacement, a 14th century stone bridge itself widened three centuries later. The chapel on the bridge dates from the same period when it became a 'blind house' or lock-up complete with two cells. The narrow, picturesque pedestrian way opposite Church Street is called The Shambles; its canopied and flower-bedecked frontages belie its origins as the original site of the town's slaughterhouses.

2 Cross the bridge, turn left up Market Street (beware the lack of footpath!) and first left along Church Street to the Saxon Church of St Lawrence.

A BRADFORD'S SAXON CHURCH's 'modern' history began as recently as 1856 when one Canon Jones looked down on the town and espied the shape of a small church hemmed in by cottages and houses. His discovery was given credence when in 1871 all vestiges of secular use had been removed and connection made with St Aldhelm and a local monastery mentioned in a deed of 705. Alterations and face-lifts notwithstanding, the tiny church exudes both charm and mystery, its bold simplicity and tenacity hard to forget.

3 Bear left by the Saxon Church and past Holy Trinity Church, crossing the river footbridge.

4 Turn right into the St Margaret's Street car park and along by the river, passing in front of the restaurant/pub and the swimming pool to join the riverside path.

Most of Bradford's riverside mills have gone; those that remain have found a new function in life. Those that know the Avon as a major navigable artery might be forgiven for wondering whether this gentle wanderer is indeed one and the same. The setting is increasingly rural and at Barton Packhorse Bridge, but for the powerful presence of the Tithe Barn on the left, entirely so.

5 Pass under the railway, following signs to Barton Farm; the path bends left to cross a small bridge then sharp right to settle to a straight course between the river (on the right) and the canal above.

The line of the canal is clearly defined atop the embankment to the south and the walker below can thus the

more easily appreciate the leakage problems that have been a recurring problem here since the canal was cut.

6 Follow the path up onto the canal, cross the swing bridge and turn right onto the path along the canal's offside.

7 Strike up to the left, into and through Becky Addy Wood and onto the road down to Avoncliff.

In an old etching of the area Becky Addy Wood rolls down to the canal at the south end of Avoncliff Aqueduct much as it does today. The trees still change their mood with the seasons but the scene they oversaw a century ago couldn't have been more different. Down the hillside from quarries at Westwood rattled a tramway; boats in the lee of the woods took on stone via the wharfside crane while on the far side of the aqueduct more stone awaited transport by rail. All that is now changed and the area normally only buzzes with activity at a weekend, the 'out-of-town' Cross Guns the main attraction.

8 Turn right onto the road down to Avoncliff, taking the path *under* the aqueduct and up onto the other side.

B AVONCLIFF AQUEDUCT is used to superlatives. It was such a bold act of genius, tinged perhaps with a little blind faith, that created this architectural and engineering masterpiece.
Today the setting is glorious and though, over the years, Rennie's original stonework has endured more than a few 'modifications', inside and out, the incredulous eye carefully censors their impact. Avoncliff is longer than its north-western neighbour, Dundas, but, some would say, less impressive ... a walk of less than three miles will satisfy the curious and it's a mere 200 miles to have a look at another similar, though longer and higher, Rennie aqueduct across the Lune at Lancaster.
Downstream from Avoncliff is the confluence of the rivers Avon and Frome while upstream two old flock mills, one either side of the river, have clearly gone their separate ways over the years.

9 Leave the Avoncliff area via the towpath back to Bradford; once past the cottages turn left down the steps into Barton Farm Country Park and head straight across to the riverside path for a better view of the northern flock mill.

C FLOCK MILLS broke up old woollen materials recycling them as stuffing for cushions, mattresses and the like. The brick and stone chimney of the restored (for residential use) southern mill stands proudly above all else as if to emphasise the mill owner's one-upmanship at changing from water to steam power ... the cheap coal for this new technology coming almost to the door via the canal. Across the river the northern mill is a sorry

sight; hemmed in by both river and railway, access today is almost impossible.

10 Continue along the riverside bearing right around the electricity sub-station and up onto the towpath by the swing bridge; turn left back to Bradford Wharf.

The tables are now turned. Gripe Wood cascades down to the canal from the south while the cut weaves its superior, albeit precarious, way above the river. A recent 'breach' here unearthed a cavernous hole on the offside which doubled back under the canal ... tread carefully!

D BRADFORD'S TITHE BARN's statistics are impressive: 168ft long with a massive timber roof supporting 100 tons of stone tiles. But even more impressive is that it has stood its ground here since the Abbey of Shaftesbury had it built in 1341. Tithes (one tenth of annual produce usually paid in kind to support the priesthood) are, of course, no longer paid but respect is and few will leave the Barn's simple but stunning space with less than a sense of wonder.

E BRADFORD LOCK is sandwiched between two wharves, the upper clearly being the more important. Here there are relics aplenty of the canal's heyday including a gauging dock (now the dry dock) where a craft's carrying capacity was gauged (by loading it with known stone weights, some of which are still around) in order to calculate tolls. The lock is numbered 14 and, like all the others, used to bear its number with pride. Long before restoration ever got this far a local enthusiast removed the cast iron number plate for safekeeping and, amid the festivities to celebrate the restoration of navigation in 1984, ceremoniously returned it to its rightful place. Within the week it was gone!

SUSTENANCE: Excluding Bradford itself there are three canal-side hostelries to choose from. Details of Bradford's restaurants, etc are on page 28.

... AND THERE'S MORE: Not surprisingly Bradford itself has much more to offer (see page 28) but an equally interesting extension to the walk is via the riverside path to the olde worlde village of Freshford, thence to Limpley Stoke and back to Avoncliff by canal.

PUBLIC TRANSPORT: Local rail timetable details for Bradford and Avoncliff Halt available on 0345 484950; bus information on Bath (01225) 464446.

TOURIST INFORMATION CENTRE: 34 Silver Street Bradford-on-Avon. Tel: Bradford-on-Avon (01225) 865797

Walk 3   6 Miles

Start: Honeystreet Bridge   OS ref: SU 104615

The Vale of Pewsey is a place of antiquity; the walk north from the canal at Honeystreet takes in some of the well-known – and some of the lesser known – landmarks in the area's pre-history.

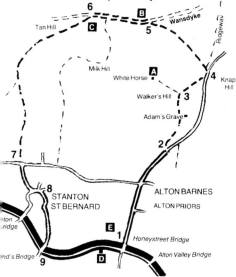

1   Proceed north along the road from Honeystreet Bridge and straight across the staggered crossroads.

Alton Barnes White Horse is clearly visible on the south-facing slope of Walker's Hill while, out of sight, off the road to the right is the tiny, almost primitive, Saxon Church of St Mary, its pulpit once occupied by the distinguished Victorian preacher and writer, Augustus Hare.

2   Turn left off the road by the small lay-by, climb the track, cross the stile and continue straight up the hill.

As the path winds round Adam's Grave, a prehistoric long barrow with part of the burial chamber exposed, a glance back offers bracing views across the Vale of Pewsey with its scattered villages and the tree-tufted summits of Woodborough and Picked Hills to the south-east. Sheep scurry across the face of Walker's Hill as if in pursuit of the fast-disappearing White Horse.

A   ALTON BARNES WHITE HORSE is a skittish creature, its high-stepping profile a landmark for miles around – indeed like all such hillside figures, it appears more in proportion from a distance. It was cut in 1812, reputedly as a copy of and competitor to the horse at Cherhill to the north-west. One John Thorne, an itinerant painter, was entrusted with the task and, upon setting others to work, made off with the 20 sovereigns in payment … Thorne was later caught and hanged for this and other misdemeanours.

3   Where the path branches, follow the right-hand

track along the dip and back down towards the road; cross the stile and turn left onto the road.

The path across the road leads up to the Neolithic encampment of Knap Hill where excavations unearthed a mass of pottery dating back to around 2000 BC.

4   Turn left off the main road via the stile and walk along the left-hand side of the field; cross the gate at the top and continue straight uphill along the slightly sunken path, crossing a second gate.

Once off the road a clearly-defined track strikes northwards towards the crest of the hill; this is the Ridgeway, a pre-historic trade route that probably ran from Axmouth in east Devon to the Wash. Today the designated Ridgeway Path runs from Overton Hill near Avebury to Ivinghoe in Buckinghamshire, an 89 mile trek that, though not always rich in the scenic sense, has a unique affinity with Mother Earth and Britain's earliest inhabitants. As the line of the Ridgeway recedes, the feeling of antiquity lingers in the sharp air; the small, almost primeval, conifered copse, the hollow scattered with large stones like some prehistoric board game and, quite suddenly, the massive embankment of Wansdyke.

5   Turn left via the stile onto Wansdyke.

B   Though WANSDYKE's origin and purpose remain obscure, it is clearly a defensive earthwork dating from the Dark Ages. Its continuous 11-mile eastern bank and ditch were protection against aggression from the north, possibly too a boundary line between Saxon allegiances. Whatever or whoever, the enigmatic legacy is the same, an impressive earthwork that affords breathtaking views in all directions.

A walk along Wansdyke offers three very different aspects – from the ditch, the lower south ridge and the high south bank. From the highest point many of Wiltshire's other antiquities are clearly visible; to the north are West Kennett Long Barrow, Silbury Hill and Avebury while to the north-west is the monument-topped summit of Cherhill. Not visible, but undoubtedly there, is the young river Kennet, winding its way round the eastern perimeter of Silbury Hill before crossing under the A4 below West Kennett Long Barrow … a trickle that is a far cry from the navigable river first encountered at Kintbury (see page 39).

6   Cross the stile and leave Wansdyke where the two rough roads meet, taking the left fork downhill between Milk and Tan Hills.

C   TAN HILL, with MILK HILL the highest in Wiltshire, used to be the site of a large and locally popular annual fair (August 6) for sheep and horses … though it was not unknown for people too to join in with the sport and merrymaking. The origins of the fair are said to date back to pre-Christian times when the Celtic pagans used the hilltop for their fire (Tan means fire) festival related to the ripening crops. Fires and fairs are no more, the memory of their magic entrusted to the wind-strewn ashes.

There are alternative paths down to the main road from Wansdyke. One winds round Milk Hill and includes the chance to seek out what is believed to be the country's oldest dewpond, Oxen Mere (first mentioned in a land survey of 825), while the track down the western sides of Tan Hill takes in the Rybury Camp hill fort on Clifford's Hill.

7   Cross the main road down into Stanton St Bernard, turning left at the church.

Like almost all the settlements along the Vale of Pewsey, Stanton St Bernard does not actually touch the canal. It is a curious blend of old farmhouses and council houses, the Victorian ashlar-faced and battlemented church leaving an impression rather than being impressive.

8   Bear right at the staggered crossroads following the road with the 'dead-end' sign out of the village towards the canal.

9   Cross Stanton Bridge and turn left onto the tow-path back towards Honeystreet Bridge.

D   THE BARGE INN is Honeystreet. True there is little left of the canalside activity that created this small settlement and which was sustained with all the basics by the inn … even if it did, prior to the disastrous fire of 1858, call itself the George Inn. In creating this settlement the canal cut across well-trodden routes, one of which, the track from Woodborough to Tan Hill Fair, was replaced here by a ferry of sorts. The so-called 'floating bridge' remained in situ for many years after the last fair atop Tan Hill in 1932.

To resist the temptation of the Barge is not easy but the end is in sight, though an ignominious end it is with the remnants of the former canal-orientated buildings looking more than a little sorry for themselves.

E   HONEYSTREET WHARF has seen better times. It is not easy to equate the rusting canopied workshops on the offside with the canal's best-known boatbuilding business, Robbins, Lane & Pinnegar. But the company did prosper not only building so-called 'Kennet' barges for the Wey Navigation and the Basingstoke Canal but also running the adjacent timber yard using their own boats to bring in raw materials from Avonmouth and Hungerford.

SUSTENANCE: Honeystreet's *Barge Inn* offers the only food and drink though it is served on a large helping of canal history.

… AND THERE'S MORE: By continuing east along the canal from Honey Street to Woodborough Fields Bridge and then turning south towards Woodborough, it is easy to pick up the track eastwards to Swanborough Tump where King Alfred wrote his will. A track north from the Tump rejoins the canal at Ladies Bridge.

PUBLIC TRANSPORT: For details of the infrequent bus services in the Devizes/Pewsey area 'phone Salisbury (01722) 336855.

TOURIST INFORMATION CENTRE: Cromwell House, Market Place, Devizes. Tel: Devizes (01380) 729408.

Walk 4   6 Miles

Start: Great Bedwyn Wharf   OS ref: SU 280644

Water is the life blood of the canal and it is in the Crofton/Wilton area that the Kennet & Avon's architect, John Rennie, sought to ensure an adequate supply.

1   Proceed south-west along the towpath to Bedwyn Church Bridge.

A   GREAT BEDWYN WHARF was, unusually, on the towpath side of the canal. In the mid-19th century it boasted two coal merchants though never generated as much trade as the nearby Burbage Wharf. Until 1915 wheat was shipped by canal from here to the mill at Aldermaston – see Walk 6, page 63.

2   Cross the gate to the left of Bedwyn Church Bridge, keeping to the right for a few yards before turning left uphill over a stile – keep the fence and the line of trees to the right.

The climb up to Castle Copse offers excellent views back across the canal. In the south-western distance is Crofton Pumping Station while to the north are the contrasting tower and spire of Great and Little Bedwyn Churches. West of Little Bedwyn's spire is the oval hill fort of Chisbury (on Wansdyke), the ramparts of which once enclosed the ancient thatched chapel of St Martin.

3   Cross the gap at the top, continuing along the right-hand side of the fields.

4   Enter Castle Copse at the top corner of the field and follow the fairly well-defined path through the wood to the clearing.

Many woodland paths are a matter of luck; an innate sense of direction helps, a compass can be a bonus. The path through the northern extremities of Castle Copse has a hit and miss quality but the intermittent dry and dank floor and the tall claustrophobic trees speed the feet towards the inevitable sunlight.

5   Fork right along the clearing and join the metalled track at is southern extremity, remaining on it as far as the southern end of Bedwyn Brail.

The sound of gunfire hereabouts is not uncommon. Despite being an endangered species, walkers need not, whatever the temptation, 'hit the floor' at the sound of each volley... it's probably too late anyway. This is pheasant country, the woods being used for pre-shooting breeding; venturing off the path is therefore, not re-commended as the motive might well be held suspect.

6   Having crossed a second gate (there are farm buildings down to the left) turn right and, ignoring the well-defined track that goes downhill, follow the line of the field opposite, keeping it as close on the left as the rampant vegetation will allow.

7   Turn left onto the bridleway – thigh-length boots are recommended in wet conditions – and then right onto the road.

B   WILTON WINDMILL is a 5-storey tower mill, built in 1821 and worked until the 1890s. Five years of restoration began in 1971 and today the mill is back in full working order, its two common (the more open) and two patent sails turning during the summer to grind flour from corn; see page 36 for opening times.

8   Turn left at the T-junction (signposted to Grafton and Burbage) and 250yds later turn right onto the Roman Road.

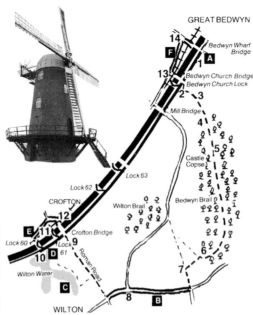

GREAT BEDWYN

Bedwyn Wharf Bridge

Bedwyn Church Bridge
Bedwyn Church Lock

Mill Bridge

Castle Copse

Lock 63

Lock 62

CROFTON

Wilton Brail

Bedwyn Brail

Crofton Bridge

Lock 60   Lock 61

Wilton Water

Roman Road

WILTON

Few designated Roman roads throw up images of marching legions; still fewer, it seems, have escaped the march of asphalt. Here is an exception. The original purpose of the Roman network of roads was military, to facilitate the advancing legions and to secure the extremities of the conquered territory. Commercial and administrative considerations followed, the road linking *Cunetio* (Mildenhall near Marlborough) and *Venta Bulgarum* (Winchester) probably having seen it all. Local lore has it that, from the road's crest, the keen-sighted could glimpse the spire of Salisbury Cathedral on a clear day; the rest of us might be content with sightings of Wilton Windmill, Crofton Pumping Station and, over on the left, Wilton Water.

9   Turn left onto the towpath towards Crofton.

C   WILTON WATER, though created artificially, has natural origins in the many local springs. The damming of the narrow branching valley was necessary to supply the much-needed water to the canal's summit level – its route being via a well under Crofton Pumping Station where it is pumped up to a leat (a narrow ditch-like channel) that carries it to an outlet above the Crofton Locks. For Wilton's abundant wildlife it's no more than a peaceful and sheltered place to be.

D   Six of the nine CROFTON LOCKS remained, for seven years from 1981, as an unrestored obstacle to navigation between the two longest navigable sections – to Devizes in the west and Newbury in the east. There would have been fewer locks to restore had an early proposal of Rennie to follow a more southerly route here been accepted. This would have created an 18-mile summit level, with the obvious benefit of increased water storage, but necessitated a costly 2½-mile tunnel ... the latter 'disadvantage' being the deciding factor.

10   Cross Lock 60 and then follow the path round to the left, then to the right and under the railway; climb the steps to the Pumping Station.

E   CROFTON PUMPING STATION was re-opened by the late John Betjeman in 1970, the culmination of several years' work by the Crofton Society. It houses two early Cornish beam engines – an 1812 Boulton & Watt and an 1845 Harvey's of Hayle – the oldest working beam engines 'in steam' in the world. Details of 'steaming' weekends, etc. are on page 36.

11   Leave the Pumping Station via the main road gate and turn right towards Crofton.

The field opposite the Pumping Station boasts a larger-than-usual pill box – perhaps the Station was considered to be of special importance. The same field now doubles as a car park, a far cry from images of the slaughter that took place here in 675 and described by the Anglo-Saxon Chronicle thus: 'in this year Wulfhere, the son of Penda, and Aescwine fought at *Biedanheafde* (Bedwyn); and in the same year Wulfhere died and Ethelred succeeded to the kingdom.'

12   Turn right where the road swings to the left and cross the railway and canal bridge, turning left onto the towpath.

The towpath walk back to Bedwyn Church Bridge is, to all intents and purposes, a typical canalside ramble. But much has changed hereabouts. The lock-keeper's cottage by Lock 62 remains but the mill that gave Mill Bridge its name is no more. The outline of Mason's Wharf can be imaginatively recreated but the nearby Bedwyn Mill has gone. The adjacent Mill House remains though it is its original name of 'Mason's Cottage' that clarifies its canal connections.

13   Turn left across Bedwyn Church Bridge, cross the railway and follow the path to the south-west of the churchyard wall, onto the main road and turn right towards Great Bedwyn.

F   GREAT BEDWYN STONE MUSEUM is owned and run by descendants of the Lloyd family who originally came from the Midlands to help build the canal – and lived in Mason's Cottage. It is an amazing place, quite unlike any other museum, and includes painted headstones and texts, fonts, statuary and fossils ... and even a do-it-yourself fountain. Details of opening times, etc. on page 36.

14   Turn right onto Bedwyn's main street – the Wharf is a few hundred yards south-east.

SUSTENANCE: Great Bedwyn has two good pubs and the *Swan Inn* at Wilton is but a short detour from the described walk.

... AND THERE'S MORE: A walk up the Crofton Locks to Wolfhall Bridge takes in the leat (where the water pumped up from Wilton enters the canal) and a few railway remnants while heading south from the bridge leads to the Tudor Wolfhall where Henry VIII met one of his wives, Jane Seymour. There are several well-sign-posted routes back to the canal, one of which takes in Wilton.

PUBLIC TRANSPORT: Details of rail services to and from Great Bedwyn are available on 0345 484950. For local Newbury Buses services, phone Newbury (01635) 40743; Wilts & Dorset also run services – phone Salisbury (01722) 336855.

TOURIST INFORMATION CENTRE: Car Park, George Lane, Marlborough. Tel: (01672) 513989.

Walk 5   6¹/₂ Miles

Start: Hamstead Bridge   OS ref: SU 424670

By definition this figure-of-eight walk can be split into two shorter walks, both of which take in snatches of the young river Kennet.

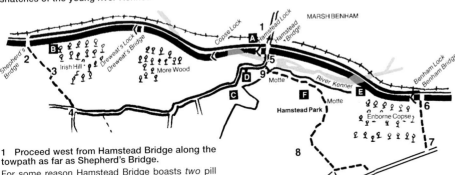

1 Proceed west from Hamstead Bridge along the towpath as far as Shepherd's Bridge.

For some reason Hamstead Bridge boasts *two* pill boxes. Such wartime relics are a feature of the whole navigation but hereabouts there seems to have been something of an epidemic – it was clearly Hitler's intention to sample the local Kennet trout for himself!

A HAMSTEAD LOCK was the first to be rebuilt west of Newbury as part of the restoration programme … at 1971 prices a snip at a mere £3000. For a few hundred yards between Hamstead and Copse Locks the river Kennet is the mainstay of the navigation but, despite the proximity of the river and its various branches, the man-made cut dominates. With the footslopes of More Wood receding, those of Irish Hill drift down to the water but are sometimes hidden from view as the towpath takes on a tunnel-like quality with tall reeds on one side and overhanging trees and bushes on the other.

B Where IRISH HILL meets the canal, east of Shepherd's Bridge, stood the last of the area's whiting mills, once the main industry of Kintbury and its environs – see page 39. The bridge itself boasts the deep time-worn grooves of countless tow-ropes.

2 Cross Shepherd's Bridge and follow the clearly defined path up the hillside.

The views back across the Kennet valley are breath-taking – and rightly so for the climb is steep and pauses for the taking of breath could well be frequent.

3 Cross the cattle grid and follow the path round to the right, keeping close to the fence. Continue straight on (where the track turns right down to the farm) and cross the stile by the lone tree – the path down to the road (the distant telegraph poles) cuts straight across the field.

Well, the map shows it going *straight* across and the stile at the other end, though out of sight, *is* in direct line … but what about the farmer's crop? Disappearing paths are a recurring problem for the seasoned walker, the answer seemingly a question of values: to cross irrespective of the type and stage of cultivation or to take a detour round the field's often endless perimeter … in this case *left* is quicker!

4 Leave the field via the stile and turn left onto the road, thereafter following all signs to Marsh Benham.

As the road approaches the crest of the hill, Dreweat's

Lock can be seen down in the valley, a black and white fingerprint nestling innocently between More Wood and Irish Mill. It's downhill all the way now … well almost.

C The EARL OF CRAVEN it was (and not Hadrian) who had that red-brick wall built around his principal seat of Hamstead Park. William Craven (1606-1697) led a remarkable life, being knighted by Charles I in 1627 and made Baron Craven of Hamstead Marshall a week later. He helped his monarch financially during the Civil War and, as the King's head rolled, was dubbed an 'offender against the Commonwealth of England'. After the Restoration Craven's popular image was as a fire-fighter, an enthusiasm that did not prevent the destruction by fire of the house in 1718. All that now remains is the wall and several pairs of entrance piers.

D ST MARY'S CHURCH clings to the high ground to the south of the road. Norman in origin, it boasts 14th-century additions and an 18th-century brick tower; the interior exudes a warmth and charm, not least from the box pews and the three-decker pulpit.

As More Wood recedes the Kennet valley once again dominates the view. The road soon drops back down, past the entrance to Hamstead Park, to river and canal, the former, not surprisingly, boasting a mill, the painted exterior of which belies its former industry.

5 Cross the canal bridge and turn right onto the towpath as far as Benham Bridge.

Across the canal the main stream of the Kennet rattles along the northern edge of Hamstead Park, camouflaged here and there by the coniferous purlieus of Enborne Copse. Contrastingly, the marshy land beyond the towpath is criss-crossed by the river's entrails and bounded by the railway embankment. Abruptly the main stream crosses the cut and in so doing creates an unusually wide waterways scene.

E BENHAM BROAD may look like a natural phenomenon – albeit with the odd sluice here and there – but it has its broad origins in another Lord Craven's desire that where the navigation crossed his estate (Benham Park) it should have an aesthetic as well as functional quality.

6 Cross Benham Bridge and over into the field, keeping to the path along the right-hand side; leave the field and cross into the lane.

7 Turn right at the top for 400 yards along the road then right into Hamstead Park opposite the church.

You have now entered an 18th-century world of running deer and tall cedars … two centuries on, the deer still roam but the now blasted cedars are almost skeletal.

8 Turn right at the first crossroads and walk round to the northern perimeter of the Park.

F HAMSTEAD PARK predates the Earl of Craven; the mounds that form its northern edge are probably the remains of the motte and bailey of the original medieval manor house, The fishpond between the two mounds dates from the same period. It is likely that William the Marshall, Earl of Pembroke and trusted stalwart of Henry II, Richard I, John and Henry III, originally established a castle on the site.

It is not difficult for the fertile imagination to recreate the impact of the embryonic canal on such an environment. The river was already a natural barrier between the Benham Park and Hamstead Park estates and local interest would soon have come to a compromise vis-à-vis the commercial benefits and aesthetic considerations. Perhaps they drew the line at the proposal of one Basingstoke entrepreneur who wanted to link the Kennet & Avon at Hamstead Marshall with Basingstoke.

9 Leave Hamstead Park and turn right onto the road and back to the canal bridge.

SUSTENANCE: The nearest hostelry is the thatched *Red House* at Marsh Benham, ¹/₄ mile north-east of Hamstead Bridge.

… AND THERE'S MORE: There are public footpaths south of the road behind Irish Hill that lead to the village of Hamstead Marshall and the *White Hart* an old country pub-cum-restaurant. From here another path cuts north-east to the southern edge of Hamstead Park and thence back to the rear of St Mary's Church.

PUBLIC TRANSPORT: For details of bus services using the A4 (about ³/₄ mile north of Hamstead Bridge), 'phone Newbury (01635) 40743. Kintbury Station is about the same distance west of Shepherd's Bridge; timetable details 0n 0345 484950.

TOURIST INFORMATION CENTRE: West Berkshire Museum, The Wharf, Newbury. Tel: Newbury (01635) 30267.

Walk 6   6¹/₂ Miles

Start: Aldermaston Lift Bridge   OS ref: SU 602672

West of Newbury the old Kennet Navigation made extensive use of the natural waters of the river; this walk sees the river both as a meandering navigation and as a many-channelled backwater.

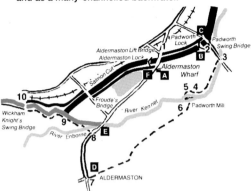

1   Proceed along the towpath between Aldermaston Lift Bridge and Padworth Bridge.

A   BREWERY HOUSE, at the south-east end of Aldermaston Lift Bridge, was once the residence of the Strange family who owned and ran the Brewery of the same name alongside Aldermaston (formerly Brewhouse) Lock opposite. The building behind also had brewing connections being the wharfside Malthouse.

It is not easy now to visualise the busy commercial activity that must once have been the norm around the wharves either side of the canal here … but, as the main transhipment area between Reading and Newbury on the old Kennet Navigation, busy it must have been. Theoretically one, the so-called Lower Wharf, still retains a semblance of 'activity' being the eastern base of British Waterways.

B   PADWORTH LOCK's contrasting brickwork is an aesthetic tribute to the restoration programme. Like most of the restored locks on the Kennet Navigation, it is a 'one off' being originally an old turf-sided lock (see page 42); boaters and walkers must decide for themselves whether they prefer the various shapes and sizes of locks at the eastern end – partially the result of sporadic rebuilding before the canal became derelict – or the conformity of the western end.

C   PADWORTH BRIDGE was, for over ten years, the limit of navigation westwards from Reading. It was one of the many swing bridges between Reading and Newbury that, almost overnight, became 'fixed' as the navigation gradually fell into disuse.

2   Turn right across Padworth Bridge and continue south.

The meandering Kennet is over to the left making its longest non-navigable impression on the landscape between Kintbury – where it first infiltrates the navigation – and Reading.

3   Cross the stile just north of the river bridge to join the riverside path to Padworth Mill.

Although today the area around Padworth Mill is an idyllic residential backwater punctuated with sluices and overspills, such mills on the Kennet predated the navigation; protection of their power sources was thus a major consideration when the river was first made navigable.

4   Cross the stile at the 'dead end' and follow the path round to the lane.

5   Turn right onto the lane and then left by the large chestnut tree (keeping to the *right* of the conifers) to cross the various sluices over the Kennet.

6   Cross the stile and follow the path straight across the field to the line of trees; cross the ditch here and turn right to follow the parallel path that leads to the rough track to Aldermaston.

The ancient village of Padworth once lay to the south, its inhabitants wiped out in the 14th century by the Black Death. The Kennet Navigation coursed its determined way through this valley with less haste and with less disastrous results, its direct approach probably bringing with it a sense of excitement and anticipation to the surrounding villages … after all, the last memorable drive this way was back during the Civil War when the Earl of Essex, fresh from victory at Newbury, led his Roundhead army to Reading.

7   Turn right at Aldermaston onto the A340.

D   ALDERMASTON ('the tun of the ealdorman') hardly seems large enough to have once supported a regular market, still less the seed of the William Pear. The local schoolmaster, John Staid, first propagated the pear, here in 1770, since when it has lost its 'Aldermaston' tag in favour of 'William'. The village also boasts an unusual triennial 'candle auction'; a candle, in which a horse-shoe nail has been set an inch below the wick, is lit to start the bidding for the grazing rights to Church Acres – the three-year rights going to the highest bidder at the moment the nail drops out. The Hind's Head inn is a 17th-century building behind which is the dome-roofed village lock-up … did one supply the other … ?

Walking north towards Aldermaston Mill gives time to reflect on the more popular image of Aldermaston gen-erated by the CND marches of the 60s and 70s. The focus of attention was Aldermaston Court which supported an establishment of the Atomic Energy Authority. Curiously today's nuclear protest focuses on another area close to the canal, Greenham Common near Newbury … perhaps all those pill-boxes are really air-shafts?

8   Turn left off the road onto the sign-posted path by a double metal gate and almost immediately right across the footbridge and head diagonally left to cross a second footbridge over the Enborne.

9   Join the riverside path by the sluices over the river Kennet and continue west along the riverside path.

E   ALDERMASTON MILL is sited at the confluence of the rivers Enborne and Kennet and, despite the loss of its original top two storeys, remains as an impressive relic of a time and way of life long gone. The Kennet was (and is) navigable as far as the mill and barge loads of corn regularly made their way down from the main channel. Formerly an hotel, the mill is today available for private functions.

10   Cross Wickham Knight's Swing Bridge and turn right onto the towpath and back to Aldermaston Lift Bridge (towpath changes sides at Froude's Bridge).

Walking along both sides of one of the longest navigable sections of the Kennet might seem like a repetitive exercise … but not so, for sounds and smells change, nature flaunts new patterns and sun and wind weave a different magic with the landscape. Not surprisingly the twists and turns rendezvous again with the branch to Aldermaston Mill and Salmon Cut, the latter's man-made directness sweeping for over a mile to Aldermaston Lock, a gem amid an otherwise drab industrial backdrop.

F   ALDERMASTON LOCK was originally turf-sided, its scalloped brickwork an innovation below the waterline; like other similar locks, it was rebuilt in the 1760s. With restoration, a feature has been made of the brickwork, the result a credit to all concerned. The adjacent information panels explain the relationship between the navigation and its surroundings, past and present.

SUSTENANCE: The *Butt Inn* is just down the road from the new lift bridge – the home-made steak & kidney pie is something special! There's also, of course, the olde worlde charm of the *Hind's Head* en route.

… AND THERE'S MORE: If the described walk is con-tinued west to Colthrop Swing Bridge and then south from the bridge, an interesting route develops round the village of Brimpton and back to Aldermaston from where the navigation can be rejoined at Froude's Bridge. En route is Brimpton Mill, a Roman road, an outbuilding at Manor Farm which was formerly the Chapel of St Leonard's used by the Knights Templar (their Maltese Cross remains over the doorway) and Shalford Farm which was used by the Knights Hospitaller.

PUBLIC TRANSPORT: Local rail information is available on 0345 484950; Newbury Buses details on Newbury (01635) 40743.

TOURIST INFORMATION CENTRE: The Town Hall, Blagrave Street, Reading. Tel: Reading (0118) 956 6226.